CREEPY *and* TRUE

MUMMIES EXPOSED!

KERRIE LOGAN HOLLIHAN

ABRAMS BOOKS FOR YOUNG READERS

NEW YORK

To young readers who ask questions and the grownups who help them find answers

Library of Congress Cataloging-in-Publication Data
Names: Hollihan, Kerrie Logan, author.
Title: Mummies exposed! / by Kerrie Logan Hollihan.
Description: New York: Abrams Books for Young Readers, 2019. | Series:
Creepy and true; #1 | Includes bibliographical references and index.
Identifiers: LCCN 2018014310 | ISBN 9781419731679 (hardcovert)
Subjects: LCSH: Mummies—Juvenile literature.
Classification: LCC GN293 .H65 2019 | DDC 393/.3—dc23

Text copyright © 2019 Kerrie Logan Hollihan
Book design by Becky James

For picture credits, see page 189.

Printed and bound in China
10 9 8 7 6 5 4 3 2 1

Abrams Books for Young Readers are available at special discounts when purchased in quantity for premiums and promotions as well as fundraising or educational use. Special editions can also be created to specification. For details, contact specialsales@abramsbooks.com or the address below.

Abrams® and Creepy and True™ are trademarks of Harry N. Abrams, Inc.

ABRAMS The Art of Books
195 Broadway, New York, NY 10007
abramsbooks.com

CONTENTS

When most people think of a mummy, they think of a body wrapped again and again in cloth, like this Egyptian mummy of a youth (80–100 AD). However, there are many other kinds of mummies.

INTRODUCTION

The invitation read something like this:

You are cordially invited to attend

the Unwrapping of a Mummy

Thursday, May 7, 1908

The Hall of Chemistry

Manchester University, England

Five hundred people—scholars and ordinary men and women—crowded into that lecture hall to watch and learn from Margaret Murray, an English archaeologist. It was the first time a woman had unrolled a mummy in front of a crowd, and her candidate was a doozy. Khnum-Nakht was one of two brothers she studied. He had lived and died during Egypt's Middle Kingdom days about four thousand years ago. A report said:

> Khnumu Nekht [as Murray spelled it] was bared of his wrappings and brought once more to the light of day . . . Near the body the linen sheets had rotted, and they fell to pieces at a touch. The bones, however, were more or less perfect. There were traces of flesh on them. It was on the whole a gruesome business, and one or two people left early.

Those one or two, and others perhaps, felt in *their* bones that Margaret Murray was working on a human being who had once been alive. They understood that Khnum-Nakht had laughed and loved, enjoyed family meals, hung out with friends, celebrated holidays, had stomach aches, and knew fear and joy . . . exactly like them. Exactly like you.

Archaeology, the study of ancient history, was a brand-new field in 1908. "Before that," Murray scoffed, "it was merely the pastime of . . . the amateur who amused himself by adding beautiful specimens to his collection of ancient art."

Murray was right. For centuries, wealthy Europeans had ventured to Egypt, coming home with mummy souvenirs to show off. And more. Artists ground mummy parts for paint to create a special tint called mummy brown. Along with

Archeologist Margaret Murray (*at table*) during a public lecture in 1908. She was likely the first woman to unwrap a mummy.

rags of all sorts, mummies went to mills to be crushed and turned into paper. Doctors prescribed powdered mummy medicine for their patients' aches and pains.

Powdered mummy? Blech! But doctors had done so for ages, possibly due to a mix-up in someone's dictionary. *Mūm* is the old Persian word for a sticky wax. It's a natural product found in oil sands and pitch lakes.

Mūm moved into other languages, and *mumia* became a term for bitumen, that smelly, gooey stuff used in asphalt driveways and parking lots. Bitumen, aka *mumia*, also served as a drug to heal all kinds of ancient ailments, from rashes to toothaches to broken bones.

Unlike mummies, languages are flexible. When folks laid eyes on Egypt's mummies, the bodies' black coating looked like bitumen, like *mumia*. (Sometimes it was bitumen; other times, it was not.) It wasn't much of a stretch to call one of these wrapped-up bodies a "mummy." Over hundreds of years, people started to believe that mummy wrappings *and* mummies themselves were powerful medicine. This belief stuck with us into the early 1900s.

Then there's the mummy's curse, another belief that's stuck around. If you've read about history's best-known mummy, King Tutankhamun (Tut) of ancient Egypt, then you might know about the curse. Within six years of Tut's discovery in 1922, at least ten people linked to the mummy died. The very first was Lord Carnarvon, the English earl who bankrolled the project to find Tut's tomb. He died of an infected mosquito bite even before he cast eyes on the mummy.

Had eager archaeologists insulted the boy king's spirit? Newspapers ran stories about "King Tut's curse," and many believed in it for years. Some still do.

When Margaret Murray died in 1963, she was one hundred years old. She saw plenty of change in her life, as humans invented and used telephones, televisions, X-ray machines, cars, and airplanes. People were dreaming of sending humans to the Moon.

Today we text on our phones, use robots for surgery, and talk about sending ourselves to Mars. Time moves on

Howard Carter and an Egyptian workman examine King Tut's third and innermost coffin of gold, which sits inside the second coffin case.

and knowledge multiplies. It's the same with archaeology. When Murray was a girl, archaeologists didn't have modern tools such as X-ray imaging, carbon dating, and DNA sampling. Since then, all these techniques have helped us to flesh out the lives of mummies.

Today in the United States, archaeology is but one branch of a much bigger field of study called anthropology. It's likely that if Margaret Murray were at work today, she'd call herself an anthropologist.

Anthropos is a Greek root word meaning human. The suffix *ology* means study.

So there you have it. Anthropology is the study of human beings and their cultures—how we live our lives—across time—from prehistoric days to the present—and across space—all around our world.

Mummies are our very best link to the past. Studying mummies is an anthropologist's dream.

Stories about King Tutankhamun abound in books and other media. No doubt about it; King Tut is Number One. But in this book, you'll meet other, equally fascinating mummies—how *they* turned up and the tales *they* tell.

Some you might know, but others will be total strangers. Some were men, others were women, and still others, kids. Some were upper crust and others, ordinary folks. Two lived and died in the past century, and the rest, from hundreds to many thousands of years ago. They turned up in Egypt, China, Central Asia, Russia, Denmark, England, Ireland, Argentina, Chile, and Peru.

But every one had a body that survived the grave, one way or another.

King Tut's glorious shoulder-length mask of gold was a crowd favorite wherever it went on tour.

FACTLET

---◆---

BODY BREAKDOWN

TO UNDERSTAND WHY mummification works, it's useful to know what happens after a person or animal dies.

ALL OF THESE HAPPEN, BUT NOT ALL AT ONCE:

- The heart stops beating.
- Blood stops flowing and begins to thicken— *livor mortis*.
- The bowels and bladder empty themselves.
- Body temperature drops, a process called *algor mortis*.
- The muscles stiffen. *Rigor mortis* sets in.
- Starved of blood oxygen, cells die.
- The skin turns blue-green.

LEFT TO THE OPEN AIR AND THE WORK OF NATURE, THE PROCESS CONTINUES:

- Decaying tissues excrete enzymes that encourage bacteria and fungi to grow.
- Bacteria produce stinky chemicals called putrescine and cadaverine, explaining why cadavers smell putrid.
- Sulphur-based compounds add to the stench. Think spoiled meat mixed with rotten eggs.
- Gases from these byproducts fill the body until it bursts.
- Soft tissues—organs and skin—disintegrate or are eaten by insects and animals attracted by the foul smell.

Sometime between fifty days and one year after death, the body enters a state of dry decay. Only hair and bones remain. In time, microorganisms will eat the hair.

Keep in mind that the warmer the temperature, the more quickly a body decomposes.

And to debunk one long-lived myth: Hair, beards, and nails do not grow after death. They might appear to, but in fact, the body shrinks. Makes sense, right?

FACTLET

AS THE AUTHOR FINISHED this book in 2018, newspapers reported a new discovery. Margaret Murray had noted that the skulls of the "mummy brothers" looked very different. Genetic tests showed that the brothers whom Murray unwrapped had different fathers. As you shall discover, there's always something new to learn about old stuff!

CHAPTER ONE

WHAT'S BEHIND CURTAIN NUMBER ONE?

IN 1988, VICTOR MAIR, AN AMERICAN PROFESSOR OF Chinese language and literature, led a tour to western China. The group was visiting a museum in the city of Ürümchi, a remote place on an ancient trading trail known as the Silk Road.

The professor and his entourage were checking out displays when he caught a glimpse of a dimly lit gallery partly hidden by a drape. He ventured in, and what he saw changed his life.

Three mummies, looking as though they were sleeping, were laid out in this quiet room. The mummies, a man, a woman, and a baby, were all dressed in bright clothes made

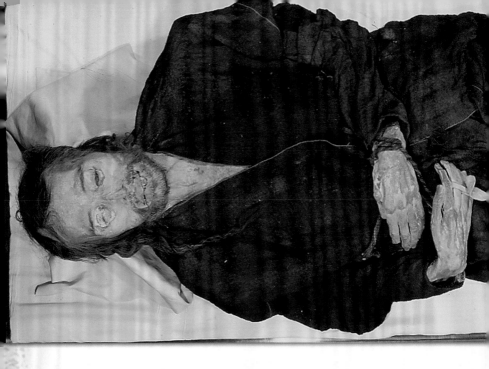

of wool and leather. The man and woman had shared a grave, and the baby had not been far off. The preservation was so incredible that at first, the professor thought they were made of wax.

But when Mair stepped in for a closer look, he realized they were the real deal. These were ancient people, their long hair and skin so well preserved they might have been freeze-dried. Their round eyes and long noses, long arms and legs, and fair hair—not to mention their overbites—made them look European. But they'd been discovered in western China, in the desert sands of a bowl-shaped place called the Tarim Basin. Out in the desert, as Mair would learn, there were hundreds more. At one time, there may have been thousands of mummies.

Ur-David, or Chärchän Man, who died about 1000 BCE, dried in a desert grave in the Tarim Basin in Central Asia.

He was, as he later said, "thunderstruck."

Professor Mair was drawn to the man because the sleeping mummy looked strangely like his own brother:

> He looked like my brother Dave sleeping there, and that's what really got me. I just kept looking at him, looking at his closed eyes. I couldn't tear myself away, and I went around his glass case again and again and again . . . I was supposed to be leading our group. I just forgot about them for two or three hours.

Mair good-humoredly nicknamed the mummy "Ur-David"—*Ur* meaning "earliest." The Chinese museum, on the other hand, had formally named him "Chärchän

Man," in honor of where he'd been found. From all appearances, he died when he was about fifty-five. He'd walked the earth about 1000 BCE. He'd been buried with a dead horse above him in the grave.

Head on pillow, Ur-David rested on his back, knees bent a bit, his long hands joined by a braided yarn strikingly similar to a friendship bracelet. He wore pants and a shirt fashioned from purple-red wool accented with red piping. White, thigh-high deerskin boots covered his knee socks of mashed-up wool, striped in bold colors of red and gold, with pale blue thrown in for eye-popping effect.

An odd-looking leather thong wrapped around the middle finger of his left hand—mysterious, to be sure. Possibly it was a form of riding crop. Back in the day, men who wore pants spent long hours on horseback. Guys who wore togas or gowns did not.

Then there was his unforgettable face. Sunken eyes, rather round, with wrinkles at the corners. A long nose, narrow and high-bridged. Mouth gently open, not the gaping scream we so often associate with mummies. A good set of teeth. Yellow spirals painted with ocher, a pigment pulled from the earth, whirled on each temple. He had lightish hair and a short beard. A red wool chin strap had slipped down over his neck. The strap probably explained why his mouth stayed mostly where it was supposed to be. He had pierced ears, with red wool threaded through them.

The woman was found buried crosswise above Ur-David. Was she his lady? A fashionista like Ur-David, and a few years younger, her painted face bore a white stripe between her eyes and tiny, bright-yellow spirals alongside her nose and on her eyelids. Skinny red triangles ran from the corners of her eyes down her cheeks. Like the man, her hands were tied with wrist cords of blue, pink, and red yarn. Her hair, which she wore in two braids, had strands of gray mixed with light brown. She'd added two more braids—blond—from someone else. Her red wool chinstrap hadn't done its work. Her mouth was open, and her tongue curled outward.

Red wool threaded through her pierced ears, as well. She was quite ladylike in a woolen dress woven with a bit of shine that just might have been silk. The armpits of her dress were open at the bottom, perhaps to let in a bit of air or to let her poke her arms out if she needed to move more freely. She, too, wore white deerskin boots, padded inside with blue and yellow felt.

The smallest member of the trio was an infant wrapped by loving hands in brown cloth held closed by red-and-blue yarn cording. The baby had been sent to the afterlife with a bottle fashioned from a sheep's udder, complete with a teat for the child to suck, though wool hid the infant's mouth from view. Tiny bits of red wool were tucked into each little nostril. (Why, no one can be sure, but it's possible the wool was meant to stop them from leaking.) Most striking were

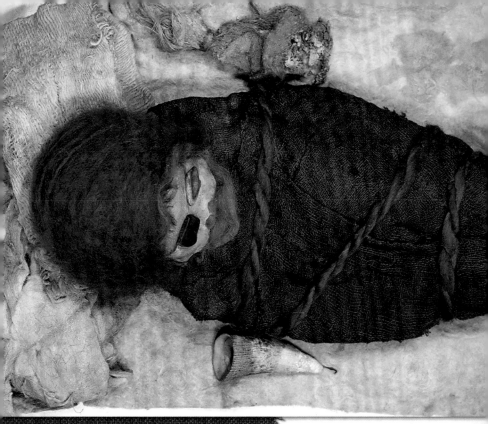

Experts do not know whether the baby buried near Chärchän Man was a boy or girl.

the bright blue hat and blue stones placed atop the baby's eyelids. Did the little one have bright blue eyes?

Professor Mair put those questions aside for a moment while he went scouting farther.

Even more mummies lay there. One caught Mair's eye, a real jaw-dropper, in mummy terms. So lovely was she that the Chinese named her the "Beauty of Loulan." Somewhere between forty and forty-five years old when she died, she lay about four thousand years waiting to be discovered.

This made her about one thousand years older than the Ur-David clan.

Living in the high desert, she'd spent a lot of time around fires—her lungs were filled with charcoal dust and sand. Beauty's skin was a reddish brown. Her blond-brown hair was wrapped in a headdress of wool felt adorned with two goose feathers. Her lovely locks were full of dead head lice. At night, the itch would have been horrific.

Beauty didn't sport the same bright clothes as the others, but her outfit hinted that she died in winter. Both her leather boots and wool skirt were fur-lined, and her overwrap was thickly woven to keep her warm. Her cap tied at the neck, another way to protect her from bitter desert temperatures in winter when the thermometer plunged far below zero.

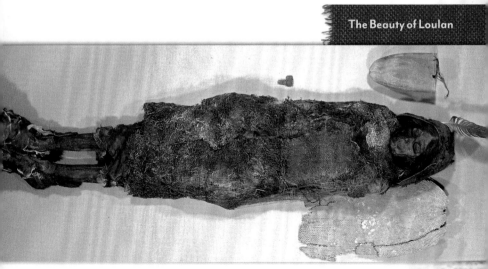

The Beauty of Loulan

Other mummies turned up from other parts of the basin. These weren't as well-preserved, but they shared Ur-David's Caucasian features. Their outfits flaunted one more surprise. Some wore soft-colored tartans, the criss-cross striped plaids on kilts worn by the Scots and the Irish even to this day. But this was in 1000 BCE!

Most of the mummies were laid to rest with useful items they'd need in the afterlife. Chärchän Man, or Ur-David, was found with a small bowl of ocher and two clay spoons to freshen his face paint. Baby Blue, of course, had its sheep's udder bottle. The Beauty of Loulan was buried with a comb—to deal with the lice, perhaps? But it well might have doubled as a weaving tool to pack threads of yarn tight together as she wove.

So there they were. These lifelike dead, with all the signs of being European imports, had been discovered in a desert basin in Central Asia—mummies in a Chinese museum looking like they should have died in Western Europe, where people were tall and fair-haired and had significant overbites, unlike the Chinese, who stood shorter and had smaller, flatter noses; fewer overbites; and dark hair. They were buried thousands of miles from what should have been home. Why were they there?

Professor Mair stashed this question in the back of his mind and went back to studying ancient Chinese writings.

But in 1991, when he read a news story about the Alpine discovery of an ice mummy, Mair changed direction. "That very afternoon, I became an archaeologist," he said. He wanted to study the mummies in detail—Ur-David, his presumed wife, the baby, and the Beauty of Loulan, plus the other mummies stashed in various states of decay in the museum and the ones still lying in their desert graves.

First, Mair had to get permission to examine the mummies, but they were pretty much a secret. Sure these Caucasian-looking dead were in a museum—but hidden behind a drape.

It was as if someone had said, "Pay no attention to that man behind the curtain."

The Chinese government had thrown up a great wall of secrecy, possibly because finding European mummies in Chinese territory was embarrassing. China has a very ancient past stretching back thousands of years. China's leaders claimed that, all that time, this great and glorious civilization grew and prospered in isolation, pure, alone, and untouched by anybody else.

But now some shovel-happy Chinese archaeologists had dug up non-Chinese mummies, giving the Chinese government a giant headache. Not to mention that the graves were discovered in extreme western China, whose locals, the non-Chinese Uighurs [WIG-gers] were quite unhappy with the government. And outsiders had come to know about the mummies, too, when the Chinese would have preferred to keep things quiet.

Nonetheless, Victor Mair convinced the Chinese that he was a good guy, worthy enough to partner with them in mummy studies. He proved his patience, too, because the Chinese government is very big, and Mair had to cut through light-years of red tape to get its permission. It helped that he spoke and wrote excellent Mandarin, China's official version of Chinese. If someone blocked his way, Mair knew how to say "我可跟你的主管人说话吗?" ("May I speak to your supervisor?")

Still, it took until 1993 for the Chinese government to give Mair permission to collect tissue samples. Mair's associate, an Italian geneticist named Paolo Francalacci, decided that still-buried but unstudied mummies offered the best testable tissue. Out to the desert they went for a visit with the dead.

Francalacci extracted twenty-five tissue samples from eleven mummies. He and Mair were prepared to fly home, samples packed, when the Chinese showed up and seized the tissues.

The disappointed professors were about to depart when a Chinese colleague appeared. In a cloak-and-dagger move, he handed off sealed samples. These five plastic vials held enough tissue for Paolo Francalacci to test and confirm that at least two of those eleven mummies shared genes with modern Europeans.

But that was just a tiny part to a giant genetic puzzle. Mair needed more proof, which meant more tissue samples. The Chinese government was changing its views about the matter, but it had started charging for mummy DNA at a hundred thousand dollars a pop. Victor Mair wasn't made of money, and time dragged until the National Natural Science Foundation of China gave him a permit to work with Chinese DNA researchers—in China. Victor Mair was included as one of the authors of a Chinese report published in 2010, which was a very big deal.

Once the DNA from twenty mummies was tested, the Chinese reported:

- All their male mummies descended from one genetic group in Europe.
- All their female mummies were of mixed ancestry, descending from two genetic groups: one from Asia, probably southern Siberia, and one from Europe.
- All three populations, European, Asian, and mixed, were very, very old—dating back ten thousand years.
- More than likely, the mummy women had mixed genes because their ancestors liked to mix things up. East meets West, so to speak.

According to Victor Mair, the first folks to settle in the Tarim Basin probably came with their flocks of sheep and goats from southeastern Europe—a very long way across Central Asia. Almost certainly these ancients interacted with Chinese people down through the years.

For instance, a now-dead language, Tocharian, was written in the Tarim Basin between 400 CE and 1200 CE.

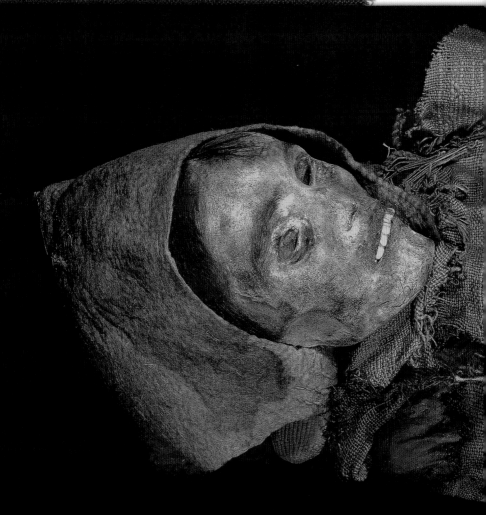

This woman, unearthed from Gumugou Cemetery in 1978, lived about 1850 BCE—some three thousand seven hundred years ago.

Tocharian is related to languages like German and Italian, but it shared at least a few words—*lion* and *honey* among them—with Chinese.

Similarly, our English word *silk* has its roots in the old Latin and Greek names for the very people from Asia who traded in this worm-spun fiber. The Latin and Greek root words for *silk* are *sēricus* and *sērikos*, "silken." The word in both languages for the silk-trading people is *Sēres*.

As Victor Mair said, an unbroken bond exists between these long-dead people and us. He spoke of them as though they were alive:

> The people of the past are people just like us—they have the same kind of desires and worries. They have symbolism, they care about their appearance—there are combs, there is mascara, [there are] mirrors. You can learn from this where we got trousers, because these people were among the first people who were wearing trousers . . . [T]hose people are all part of the big human family and our lives have been impacted by them.

So the truth that links ancient Asians and Europeans *has started* to come out, after all. But the whole truth? Stick around. **MORE MUMMY NEWS IS SURE TO COME . . .**

. . . MORE TO COME STARTS NOW
THE WITCHES IN DITCHES

Certain mummies of the Tarim Basin looked ready for trick-or-treating. Up in the northeast corner of this desert bowl, researchers unearthed three female mummies with tall pointed hats. One had double points. All three mummies looked so much like our own Halloween broom fliers that the researchers nicknamed them the "Witches of Subeshi," after a nearby town.

Their nickname turned out to be a smart choice. Victor Mair's long years of toil and trouble with the Chinese language gave him an idea. An old Chinese word, *myag* (magician), sounded a lot like *magus*, an old Persian word for magician. You'll also find *magus* in an English dictionary.

A Subeshi mummy sports a witch's hat.

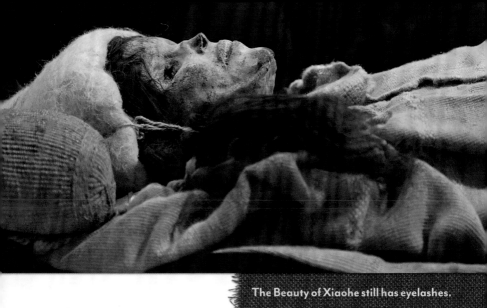

The Beauty of Xiaohe still has eyelashes.

Mair also knew that ancient Chinese *and* ancient Middle Easterners *and* modern Europeans all drew pictures of pointy-hatted individuals with special powers, which means that the Subeshi witches could possibly have been magi (plural for *magus)*.

Yes, possibly you've heard that word before.

THE BEAUTY CONTEST

Another mummy excavated in 2003 rivaled the Beauty of Loulan. She is the Beauty of Xiaohe [SHEOW-HUH], who lived and died sometime between 1800 and 1500 BCE. Her eyelashes survived the centuries, as did her tasseled, white woolen cloak, felt hat, string skirt, and leather-and-fur boots. She took along several wooden pins and three pouches of ephedra, an herb with energizing powers, for her trip through the afterlife.

Yingpan Man wore a mask that bore facial features of the local population, but underneath this Caucasoid was dressed like an ancient Greek.

THE MASKED MAN

When a man died sometime between 100 CE and 300 CE, his undertakers made him one of the best-dressed corpses ever. "He's the most resplendently garbed mummy I've ever seen, which is saying a lot for a six-foot-six guy with a mustache!" Victor Mair said. The man's face was covered by a mask crossed with a strip of gold foil, its painted face quite Asian.

But underneath, the dead man looked like a Caucasoid, a European with brown hair. Between age twenty-five and thirty, he wore a red robe embroidered in yellow. A perfume holder was tucked into his satin sash.

Chinese archaeologists named him Yingpan Man after the long-gone city where he turned up. Surprisingly, Yingpan Man was decked out as a Hellene. The Hellenes, aka Greeks, lived thousands of miles west of China.

FACTLET

IN 2009, RESEARCH ON dried-out pottery hinted that ancient Botai people first domesticated horses in Central Asia. The Botai lived fifty-five hundred years ago in modern-day Kazakhstan. Wild horses called tarpans roamed there for eleven thousand seven hundred years—until they died out in the twentieth century. Did the Botai tame the wild tarpans? Archaeologists suspected so, because they had already found multiple horse jaws damaged from bits in their mouths.

Biochemical studies of Botai pottery revealed fat from mares' milk. The archaeologists were satisfied that the Botai had indeed tamed the tarpan.

Stay close. More studies are under way in Ukraine, Spain, and Portugal. It's possible that horses were domesticated even earlier. Time will tell.

FACTLET

HERE'S THE WORD *mummy* in traditional Chinese:
木乃伊
Pronounce it MU-NAI-YI.

CHAPTER TWO

THE MOCHE MOMMY AND MANY MORE MUMMIES

ABOUT 450 CE, A GROUP OF PEOPLE LAID A BELOVED leader to rest in a temple built of bricks. It's a place called *El Brujo*, the Wizard.

But the hills rising above the desert along Peru's northern coast are no wizard's hideout. They're part of a landscape of pyramids, the giant adobe temples of the Moche [MO-chay] people, who lived there from about 100 CE until 750 CE. In these working temples, the high priests of the Moche hung out and conducted their ceremonies of life and death. There, the Moche interred their special dead.

The Moche elite were buried in tombs among the adobe bricks, sealed in, and forgotten. Outside, as time went on, the pyramids grew up and around the tombs, with add-ons of porches, patios, workplaces, and ceremonial spaces. Inside, the graves got wet, or the seals broke, and Mother Nature stepped in to do her thing with the bodies, turning them to slime and dust and bones.

The naked body of one particular Moche was decorated and wrapped in a giant bundle of cloth. But rain never seeped into its tomb. Its seals stayed intact beneath a covered porch, not to mention six layers of brick, a mat, and a bunch of tree trunks. And so this Moche corpse dried out inside its bundle, folds and folds of cotton cloth wrapped around a treasure trove of bones, skin, hair, and gold.

There it waited, silently, until 2005, when some very shocked anthropologists found the grave.

It took eight men to lift the body bundle. First, however, they had to exhume its companion, the skeleton of a half-grown girl, a servant perhaps. (She'd been strangled and sent along as company for the afterlife, the executioner's cord still around her neck.)

The eight pallbearers carried the mummy bundle to the exam table. The cloth wrap made the bundle look like a giant burrito, but it bore something unusual: a face neatly stitched in thick yarn. There were two big eyes, a nose, and a crooked smile, along with a pair of ears and a unibrow running across the top.

A textile expert did the unwrapping. She took her time, peeling away thin strips of fabric, hundreds of yards of it. It took two months of work, seven days a week.

All that time, an American anthropologist named John Verano and a photographer waited to take pictures of whatever was inside the bundle. Then time ran out; they had other assignments. They were packing their bags, thinking they'd missed a great opportunity to see inside this mysterious bundle, when they got the call. The body had been exposed—not bones—a mummified body.

They grabbed their cameras and hustled to the site. "Dumbfounded," Professor Verano said later. "Impressed. We looked at it and just went 'Wow.'"

Surprise! The Moche didn't mummify their dead. Yes, the Moche buried their honored ones in tombs, along with everything for the afterlife—weapons, tools, and other people to wait on them. Regular folks went into graves as well, holding humble things like sticks or bits of clay pots.

A golden bowl covered the head of the body Professor Verano viewed—not what one would expect to see on a fifteen-hundred-year-old corpse. Under the bowl, the face was painted with earthy red cinnabar. It had the color and texture of the crust on a nicely baked brownie—almost as though you could crack it with a fingertip.

Straight brown bangs fell into its eyes, or what would have been eyes in about 450 CE. A nice set of teeth, too, clean and straight. Lips? They curled back in a kind of snarl.

And there was one more detail that shocked everyone in the exam room. In Moche culture, it was a man's world—or so went the thinking. But this VIP burial was of a woman.

Girl power, Moche style.

Household items like spindles and needles and weaving materials were buried with her—the practical things a woman would need to get her work done. So were dresses to wear—not on the mummy but wrapped in her bundle. That extra pair of hands—the young girl—would have served her in the afterlife. (The rope that strangled her also supplied the material to carbon date the burial.)

But there was more to see in that tomb, and it astonished everyone who laid eyes on the mummy, whom they named the Lady of Cao.

A golden bowl covered the face of this mummy.

She had a pair of ceremonial war clubs wrapped in gold; twenty-eight spear throwers with fanciful designs; two towering headdresses—men's headdresses—that could have come as gifts from adoring visitors; plus fifteen necklaces, including a heavy strand of gold-and-copper beads fashioned into tiny faces.

And nose ornaments. Not those slim, delicate piercings you see today. We're talking huge ornaments of beaten silver and gold that hung from both nostrils like a giant moustache. Ornaments engraved with all manner of warriors and condors biting at human heads. What was more, the Lady was interred with a quartet of crowns, each one bearing its own fanged face.

Hair and skin intact, the Lady of Cao wore a pair of braids that ran below her boney shoulders. She was perfectly preserved from the top of her head to the tips of her tattooed fingers and toes. Inky-blue snakes and spiders and crabs and

The Lady of Cao rules as an example of a natural mummy.

The Lady of Cao has tattoos snaking down her arms.

cats ran down her arms and her long, elegant fingers. The skin of her belly was shriveled somewhat, a sign that she'd given birth at least once. She'd probably died in her late twenties, but not one clue on her body explained why.

A woman! Her culture was a man's world, or so the experts thought, but this Moche *muchacha* must have ruled. She was buried with weapons. Was she a warrior queen? Or did she serve as a priestess? Something was up. Why else would the lady be buried with such pomp and circumstance?

All these questions were thought provoking, and archaeologists and scientists have been thinking about the Lady of Cao ever since. Her discovery turned their theories about the Moche upside down. Again, there's always something new to learn about something old.

MORE ON MOCHE

Other Moche burials of women turned up before the Lady of Cao appeared, but as you might expect about typical burials in that part of the world, they aren't mummies. None outshines the Lady of Cao, whose status in that part of the archaeology world is rivaled only by . . . the Lord of Sipán.

Almost twenty years before the Lady of Cao was found asleep in her tomb, a bunch of grave robbers struck gold and more when they tunneled into another mud-brick pyramid near Peru's coastal city of Chiclayo. Sacks of their loot appeared on the black market, but for some reason, the looters got into a fight. There is no honor among thieves, and one grave robber turned snitch and called the cops.

A gunfight ensued, and once the cops won, they let in the experts who stood by watching the drama. They all picked their way through the robbers' tunnel and discovered lots more the robbers hadn't found, including a gilded copper mask and two copper scepters.

Then they happened onto a secret chamber filled with thirteen hundred pieces of pottery—which is a good-size pile of ceramics—and a second tomb. Inside lay the body of a Moche man.

The Lord of Sipán's grave claimed top billing among South America's ancient burials—until the Lady of Cao's grave was unearthed in 2006.

This fellow seemed as impressive as King Tut. So grand was his grave, the experts gave him the title Lord of Sipán. Decked out in a gold face mask, gold and silver beads, a gold knife, and a two-pound gold shield, he held court in his tomb. Seven others were buried with him. There were three young women, a young boy, two men, and a guard with amputated feet—to ensure he stayed at his post? Plus a dog—the family pet?

To be sure, this mighty lord was the king of *machismo* among all the ancient burials in South America. But the Lord of Sipán was all bones. The Lady of Cao was all skin *and* bones, which raised her to that more refined class of natural mummies.

CHILE'S CHINCHORRO

Even older than the Lady of Cao were the Chinchorro mummies of Chile. Centuries before the Lady of Cao was sealed away under all those clay bricks, an older group in South America made mummies on purpose. We call those folks the Chinchorro, and they lived in the Atacama Desert, one of the most desolate spots on earth.

The Chinchorro rose out of that desert eight thousand years ago. They lived along the edge of hills of sand that border southern Peru and northern Chile, right where the South American west coast curves eastward. Bands of hunter-gatherers, the Chinchorro scraped out their living as fishermen. Their culture hadn't advanced far enough for them to make pottery or to weave, but the Chinchorro did succeed in one art form: They learned to mummify, thousands of years before Egyptians worked out their process. That makes the Chinchorro mummies the oldest on earth.

Why did they start mummifying? It's possible the Chinchorro believed in life after death. "Artificial mummification provided a resting place for the soul, and therefore the mummies were considered living entities [beings]," wrote Bernardo Arriaza, a Chilean anthropologist.

Archaeologists think that climate change might provide a second answer. Sometime around 6000 BCE, the climate eased up on the Atacama Desert. It was still a desert, but it seems that the Chinchorro had an easier time of it for a few thousand years. When the climate changed again and desert life turned very tough, the mummifying stopped. If you're preoccupied with grubbing out a life in the desert, you have no time for leisure tasks.

When the Chinchorro made mummies, they used simple methods, and at first, the results were very basic. The Chinchorro cleaned out a corpse of its heart, lungs, stomach, and more. They tore muscles away from bones and added sticks to keep the bones straight. The dead person's skin—or animal skin, when more was needed—went back on. They finished by painting the whole thing with a mineral that turned the mummy black. A simple mask and a wig of human hair stuck on with a mud hat put the icing on the cake, so to speak. The Chinchorro even added hair extensions.

As their skills improved over the centuries, the Chinchorro turned out red mummies stuffed with clay, feathers, fur, and plants. Wigs were longer, and masks, fancier. Others of their dear departed were eviscerated and wrapped in strands of vegetable fiber. More were cleaned out but didn't get any special treatment except a cover of mud.

The Chinchorro mummified *a lot*. We know this because Chinchorro mummies turn up everywhere. Walk into the Atacama Desert, and you'll find it strewn with bones and corn cobs and rocks they built their huts on. Chinchorro cemeteries are everywhere. They buried the dead in shallow graves—which makes total sense if you've ever tried to dig a deep hole in dry sand. The dry air and wind and the sand itself helped protect them. "Once you die, you naturally mummify," said a Chilean ecologist. "Because it's very dry, corpses do not decompose. So you stick around."

And stick around they did. For those three thousand years when life was good, the Chinchorro mummified everybody, from old people to unborn babies. So there were mummies *everywhere*. Do the math: If a new generation comes along every twenty years, and you make mummies for three thousand years, that's fifteen thousand generations of mummy making.

With all those mummies, it struck the archaeologists that these dead played a living role in Chinchorro life. Maybe they started the afterlife not in graves, but hanging out with the living in their huts and villages. Maybe, the experts thought, the Chinchorro believed that the soul of a dead person needed its former body as a resting place, so they kept their dead close by.

About 2000 BCE, along came climate change again. The desert got drier and fishing harder, and so the mummy making stopped. Archaeologists think the Chinchorro left the seaside and headed for the Andes Mountains in search of a better life. They disappeared and never were heard from again.

This Chinchorro child, the oldest mummy pictured in this book, lived as long as seven thousand to eight thousand years ago.

FACTLET

ARCHAEOLOGISTS LAID THEIR HANDS on Moche pottery, goldwork, and textiles well before they found any Moche graves. The ceramic pots, engraved metalwork, and weaving showed graphic pictures of Moche life—or so they supposed. Scenes of war, prisoners forced to march, and a hideous "sacrifice ceremony" of execution and drinking blood all appeared on Moche handicraft. The pictures told all kinds of stories, but were the stories true?

Once the graves appeared, their occupants told the tale. The experts were astounded to find bodies dressed the very same as in images of people in Moche art. "When the sacrifice ceremony was first identified in Moche art . . . no one could be sure it was a real practice, as opposed to a mythical event," said one. "Now we had archeological evidence that this was an actual part of Moche life. Here was one of the individuals who presided over the sacrifices." And whose grave helped tell the tale? None other than the Lord of Sipán.

"We had identified him in 1972, but we thought he was mythical," said archaeologist Christopher Donnan. When he laid eyes on the corpse, Donnan thought, "Wait a minute, I know who that is."

Wrinkle Face, a Moche god, often appeared on Moche pottery. This is an example of a sacrificer scene bottle. Wrinkle Face's victim's head and body lay at his feet.

FACTLET

SOME MOCHE CORPSES were devoured by the likes of beetles and blowflies, invited to dine on a loved one before the burial. One researcher suggested the Moche hoped that feasting flies and maggots would transport the spirit of the dead into living flies—and on into human contact. This we suspect because a Moche mask sports a tattooed necklace of flies, and a necklace of pupating flies appeared on at least one piece of pottery. (Ancient cultures usually didn't take the time to draw something unless it was important.)

As one might expect, other experts disagree.

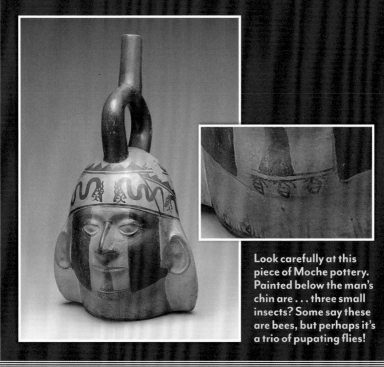

Look carefully at this piece of Moche pottery. Painted below the man's chin are . . . three small insects? Some say these are bees, but perhaps it's a trio of pupating flies!

CHAPTER THREE

ÖTZI THE ITALIAN ICEMAN

ON THE MORNING OF SEPTEMBER 18, 1991, A GERMAN couple, Helmut and Erika Simon, set their sights on a mountaintop in the Austrian Alps named Similaun. For experienced hikers such as the Simons, the summit was well within reach of a day's climb. The middle-aged couple followed in the footsteps of scores of hikers who had made this trek.

High up the mountain, they came to a glacier, Niederjochferner [nee-der-YOCK-fair-nair]. They stopped to put crampons—long spiked plates that would keep them from sliding—on the soles of their boots and picked their way across. Like most glaciers in these warmer times, this one was melting, retreating uphill. Still, the glacier, laced with dangerous crevasses, slowed them down. Once they walked off its slick, icy surface, they were an hour behind schedule. The Simons decided to spend the night at a mountain lodge. They finished their climb to the peak, snapped some pictures, and began the return trip to the chalet. They wandered away from the trail, where the melting glacier had exposed rocky, barren soil. They were still quite high, some ten thousand five hundred feet (thirty-two hundred meters) above sea level.

"*Schau mal, was da liegt*" ("Look what's there"), Helmut said. They spotted an odd shape poking out of a pool of ice and slush. They drew closer and saw a shape frozen stiff. It looked strange, like a dead animal, but the Simons quickly grasped that they'd stumbled upon a real stiff, a dead guy face down and freeze-dried. Its top half, exposed to the air, sprawled across a large flat rock, but its hips and legs were encased in ice. The corpse was naked and flat, smashed into a mass of skin and bone. Each rib was visible along a bumpy spine. This random discovery, so unexpected, shocked the Simons.

Helmut snapped a picture of the corpse. Surely, he thought, a family existed who should know how its loved one had met a terrible end. Death on the mountain was common; unwary hikers fell into crevasses all the time. Oft-told tales spoke of bodies showing up decades after hikers disappeared, their bodies dragged along as the ice moved at its glacial pace.

The Simons reported their find at the lodge. Their host, a mountain man himself, called the police. He and a friend headed up the next day to look.

At the scene, the young men started to poke around. They found a stone-bladed knife and an ax, handcrafted with a metal head, strapped to a tree branch. Strings, fur, sticks, and boards were strewn about. These objects were old—so old they couldn't belong to anyone modern. "How old would be astonishing," said Patrick Hunt, an archaeologist who later studied the mummy.

The investigation launched. There were rules for recovering the dead from high in the Alps. On the third day, a helicopter landed on the mountain, and the process began. An Austrian inspector started chipping away at the frozen carcass with a small jackhammer. He planned to finish the job and take the corpse back with him.

But it was tough work. The inspector was belly down on the ice, his arm underwater. He couldn't see clearly, and sometimes the jackhammer may have bit into the corpse, possibly ripping at its hip. Then the machine quit, so the corpse stayed put.

News of the discovery trickled down the mountain and hit the papers. People who follow these kinds of stories got excited when they heard about the tools made of stone. A champion mountaineer, nearby on an Alpine tour, hiked over. Another hiker, an author and student of mountain lore, turned up, too. The mountaineer was keen on preserving the mountain wilderness; the author, on uncovering its hidden stories.

The mountaineer told a reporter that the corpse was prehistoric. He guessed its age at between five hundred and three thousand years old. The ax told the author a story, too—its head was reputedly copper, and copper hadn't appeared in ax-heads for a very long time.

Mountaineers Reinhold Messner and Hans Kammerlander trekked to view Ötzi, who had been frozen in a glacier high in the Italian Alps.

Those first few days, matters moved at glacial speed. No one took charge. Nor, for that matter, could anyone be sure what the Simons had stumbled on: accident site, murder scene, or archaeological wonder.

Five days after the discovery, another helicopter landed, carrying an expert from the forensic-medicine institute at Austria's University of Innsbruck. He was tasked with recovering the corpse.

A pickax and ski pole helped to free the icebound body. None too delicately, the frozen corpse was lifted from the ice and flipped on its back. Its right arm lay stiff at its side, the left thrown across the chest. Its face was squished flat; the upper lip curled back. Its eyeballs were there, a remarkable sight.

Groups of short blue lines adorned its skin, the second layer of skin, that is. The epidermis, the outer skin layer, was gone. (This happens when bodies sit in water a while.) But the corpse had already scored a big-time honor: With skin intact, it qualified as one of the world's few ice mummies.

The dead man—if he were a man—looked disgusted at the whole affair.

Zipped into a see-through body bag, the frozen corpse was airlifted to the waiting hands of an undertaker. He shoved the corpse into a pine coffin and took it by hearse to Innsbruck, where a medical examiner stood by. The examiner bypassed the usual autopsy but gave the corpse a physical.

Konrad Spindler, the University of Innsbruck's top archaeologist, checked in. His take on the corpse and his gear—especially the unique ax—chilled everyone. This very corpse that someone had tried to jackhammer out of the ice? It wasn't four hundred years old. Spindler suspected that the man had been dead at least four *thousand* years. "And if the dating is revised," he added, "it will be even earlier."

Hours had passed. The warming body needed a frozen home. Luckily, an anatomy professor had an empty freezer on campus.

The researchers froze the corpse in high humidity at 21 degrees Fahrenheit (-6 degrees Celsius). In those condi-tions, they hoped, the corpse wouldn't rot. To make sure, the researchers wrapped it in carbolic-soaked cloth. Car-bolic, which smells a bit like hot tar, is a sweetish, poisonous acid. It was sure to kill any bacteria or mold that the corpse picked up during its hasty trip off the mountain.

MOUNTAIN MUMMY MYSTERY

Word of the ice mummy snowballed, and the frozen corpse became a media star. Some reporters called him Iceman. Others tagged him Ötzi, for the Ötztal Alps where the

Simons had discovered him. (In German, the *ö* in Ötzi is spoken like an *oe* sound. The closest we English speakers can come is to rhyme *Ötzi* with *tootsie*.) Headlines followed and got people talking:

Scientists Enthralled by Bronze Age Body

They got the Bronze Age part wrong.

Should Just Anybody Be Allowed to Stare?

Is it wrong to put dead people on display in museums?

Lessons in Iceman's Prehistoric Medicine Kit

Not just bodies—plants also help solve medical mysteries.

At first, the authorities assumed he was Austrian, given the spot they'd checked on a climbers' map. But a few years later, the Italians checked their maps by GPS (Global Positioning Satellite) and decided that Ötzi had turned up on Italian territory. They demanded that Ötzi be handed over. Fighting over the land had gone on for years, and überpatriots on both sides claimed Ötzi for themselves. Ötzi became a political soccer ball, as arguments bounced back and forth over the border between Austria and Italy.

The researchers in Austria begged for more time to finish their Iceman studies. Some had grown quite protective of their ice mummy. There was money to be made from books, videos, grants from wealthy donors, speeches to a curious public. Ötzi was a celebrity, and where celebrities go, dollars (or euros) would flow.

The Austrians uncovered an avalanche of information. Using carbon dating on some of the plant material at the site, they approximated Ötzi's age: fifty-three hundred years old. Ötzi was a Copper Age fellow, who lived in the late Neolithic period, when the Stone Age gave way to the Bronze Age. Ötzi had trekked the Ötztal range about 3000 BCE.

The Iceman had stood five feet two inches tall (1.6 meters) and weighed about one hundred ten pounds (50 kilos). They X-rayed him and took CAT (computerized axial tomography) scans, which revealed Ötzi head to toe in "slices," like a loaf of bread.

The researchers wondered about the stuff Ötzi carried. They returned to the site and found a wealth of evidence. A stone-bladed knife, a bearskin hat (fur side in), bits and pieces of a long fur coat, a cape fashioned from grass or reeds, a loin cloth, and leggings attached to Ötzi with a belt and leather garters. (His leggings had peeled off his legs when he was hoisted from the ice.) Ötzi had blood on his clothes, not all of it his.

Pieces of hide and wood bent into a frame hinted that Ötzi had carried a pack. From the ice, his finders also pried a long stick, thought to be a walking staff until an archaeologist identified it as a longbow. Like Ötzi's ax, the longbow was made of wood from the yew tree, the very best possible

This model of Ötzi shows him as a tired, aging hunter. The model is on exhibit in the museum that houses the Iceman's body.

for crafting this lengthy weapon. There was a quiver filled with arrows, two of them tipped with stone arrowheads.

Both impressed the experts. The longbow was of the same design as the legendary bows shot by England's archers during the Middle Ages. ("Think Robin Hood and the battles of Crécy and Agincourt," said Patrick Hunt.) Ötzi's people understood aerodynamics. The arrows were fletched in spirals—set into the wood—so that the arrows would fly straight and true like a well-thrown football.

Ötzi still wore one shoe made of calfskin, grass, and string. He carried a bit of food, including dried sloeberries to boost his energy—and two kinds of mushrooms. "Why the fungi?" they wondered.

It was simple luck that the Iceman still looked like a man. Other glacier corpses routinely showed up flattened like griddlecakes or transformed into a smelly material that resembles Styrofoam. But Ötzi had died in a trench in the ground. Layers of snow and ice had piled on top of him, but as the glacier ground across the valley, it skimmed over Ötzi's gully grave.

One expert guessed that Ötzi had stopped to sleep high on the mountain and froze to death. "He died quite peacefully," he said. Nevertheless, other archaeologists, including the team leader, disagreed. He theorized that Ötzi was a herdsman who'd brought his flock of sheep and goats off the mountain to winter in the valley. There, Ötzi had gotten into a fight, and he began climbing to get away from his enemies. High on the mountain, he stopped to rest, and there he died.

More scientists flocked to study the Iceman and his gear. They learned lots more. Ötzi wrapped both his food and hot embers for starting campfires in big leaves. The embers, covered to burn slowly, could be carried in his backpack for days if need be. The fungi had served two purposes. Ötzi would have used one type that burned easily to light fires. The other, birch bracket fungus, fights bacteria and viruses. Ötzi must have used it to treat any wounds.

Down the road, experts studied Ötzi's bone marrow and found that he had Lyme disease. Like today's victims, Ötzi could have been horribly dizzy. Birch bracket fungus helped relieve that, too.

And that was that. For the moment, the experts thought they'd pretty much discovered all there was to know about the Iceman.

Ötzi, a hot commodity, was moved across the border in a secure operation to keep him safe from kidnappers. Italy welcomed him to a brand-new museum in the mountain city of Bolzano. Ötzi was entombed in a million-dollar freezer, still at 21 degrees Fahrenheit and nearly 100 percent humidity. His new caretakers wanted to protect Ötzi from freezer burn, like an aging, frozen piece of meat.

The freezer had a small window, through which visitors could view Ötzi lying in a frozen state. Outside was a dim room, a mark of respect to a once-living member of the human race.

Ötzi became a tourist attraction, and his newfound fame translated into euros for the locals. His name and portrait appeared on pizza, candy, bakery goods, and T-shirts. Candy makers couldn't keep up with the demand for Ötzis crafted from chocolate, marzipan, and nuts.

HIGH TECH, BETTER SPECS

Ten years after Ötzi arose from the ice, a radiologist took a fresh look at old scans of the Iceman. In 2001, he observed a white spot near one of Ötzi's ribs that others had missed.

The white spot turned out to be a stone arrowhead. The cutting-edged piece of flint hid deep in Ötzi's shoulder. Clearly, he'd been shot from behind. Ötzi became the oldest, coldest homicide case ever.

The Iceman again became a hot topic. Like detectives trying to catch a killer from long ago, Ötzi's examiners had to wait for technology to catch up and answer their questions. In 2005, a newly developed multislice CAT scanner did the trick, picking up much finer details inside Ötzi. The X-ray experts' report, written the way scientists write for one another, went like this:

> Historic records highlight the fatal destiny of subclavian artery injuries e.g. due to massive active bleeding and shock-related cardiac arrest. Therefore, the Iceman's cause of death by an arrowhead lacerating among others the left subclavian artery and leading to a deadly hemorrhagic shock can be now postulated with almost complete certainty.

In other words, the experts now thought that Ötzi was shot with an arrow, and the arrowhead pierced an artery beneath his left collarbone. He had bled so much that his heart stopped.

Those multislice scans dished up another surprise. The same radiologist who discovered the arrowhead had kept at it, poring through CAT images of Ötzi. Months later, he questioned the "big, hollow organ" in Ötzi's chest. It was the Iceman's stomach, shoved upward behind his ribs.

Early autopsy results were wrong. Those first explorations of Ötzi's insides had led researchers to Ötzi's colon—his large intestine. So what was in his stomach? And why was his stomach in his chest?

The first question was put on ice. Ötzi was frozen at the time, so another dig into his stomach for a food sample wasn't happening. But the experts answered the second quickly. Obviously, the ice and snow that flattened Ötzi had forced his stomach north.

COLD CASE. THAWED?

By 2010, researchers got permission to do a new autopsy of the Iceman. Ötzi was brought out of freezing conditions in a special mold that cradled his thawing body. Like a sick patient with low immunity, the Iceman couldn't spend much time in others' company.

Teams of scientists wearing caps and gowns plucked miniscule samples from his corpse. Deep from a bone they extracted material, hoping it would hold more of Ötzi's prized DNA. From head to toe, Ötzi was reexamined.

Doctors looked in Ötzi's brain to see if a shadow on an earlier scan might be a blood clot. A pinpoint-size sample

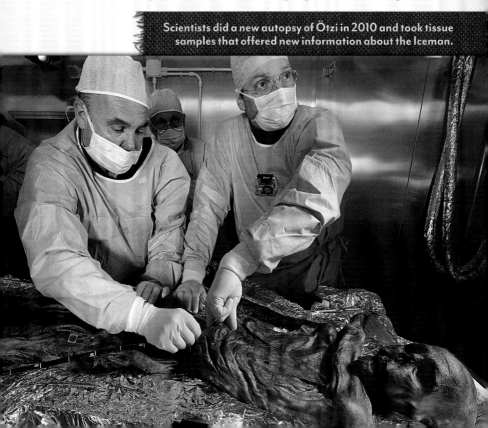

Scientists did a new autopsy of Ötzi in 2010 and took tissue samples that offered new information about the Iceman.

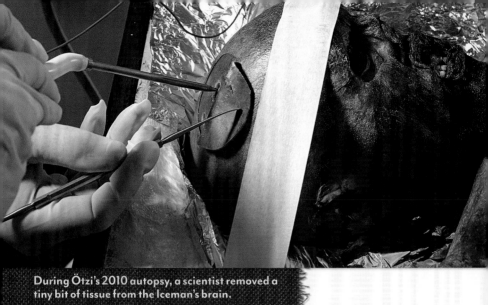

During Ötzi's 2010 autopsy, a scientist removed a tiny bit of tissue from the Iceman's brain.

of brain tissue revealed a distinct kind of protein molecule. Typically, this protein develops with bruises and blood clots—such as when someone is hit on the back of the head. Whether Ötzi fell back and banged his skull—or someone else gave it a whack—was anybody's guess.

One team went after the arrowhead, too, but they couldn't reach it without doing more damage to the mummy. Ötzi was a national treasure, and the doctors couldn't make new incisions without express permission, which they didn't have.

The Ötzi extracts, one hundred forty-nine different samples, yielded amazing results. One expert pulled out about half his stomach contents with a spoon, about the same amount as a Quarter Pounder, no cheese. Looking like pale coffee grounds, the digested material was identified as both meat and wheat. (For the record, food stays in your stomach about one hour.) The ingesta (what Ötzi ate) was passing through his gut as he died.

The examiners took chunks from Ötzi's small and large colon in four more spots. They found two kinds of tree pollen in Ötzi's intestines, some from hornbeam trees and some from conifers—evergreens. The presence of much tree pollen proved that Ötzi had died in the spring.

The Iceman's feces revealed what Ötzi ate during his last thirty-three hours on earth. And likely *where* he ate it. Microscopic pollen appeared in Ötzi's gut in sequence, first conifer pollen, then hornbeam pollen, and then more conifer pollen.

Pollen was solid evidence that Ötzi had been traveling about two days before he died. Hornbeam trees live in Alpine valleys at milder temperatures than hardier conifers, which grow at high altitudes. Above the timberline, trees cannot grow. The pollen deposits in Ötzi's bowels indicated he'd eaten on a mountain trail among evergreen trees, and again later in the valley where hornbeams grew.

Ötzi then returned to the mountain, where he ate that final feast. He climbed even farther toward Similaun, perhaps to hide from his enemies. And there, where no trees grew, Ötzi was murdered.

This was new information for the experts to digest. If Ötzi knew he had enemies in hot pursuit, would he have stopped to eat a big meal?

DNA COMES INTO PLAY

Even as Ötzi stayed frozen, the science of genetics made a great leap forward in the 1990s. Geneticists began mapping the human genome, based on their knowledge of DNA. Each of us has a genome, and it's only one-tenth of one percent different from someone else's. (Think about that: You and Ötzi share 99.999 percent of your genome.)

When Ötzi was thawed and autopsied in 2010, researchers removed bits of fat and muscle from him, along with enamel from a tooth in his right jaw. In the lab, they extracted DNA from these tiny samples in order to sequence it—map it out gene by gene.

In 2011, they began to report their findings. Ötzi had brown eyes, for one. He was lactose intolerant, too; drinking milk would have upset his stomach. The Iceman's DNA showed that he'd been infected with *Borrelia burgdorferi*, the bacteria that cause Lyme disease. He had hardening of the arteries, too. Had he not been murdered, Ötzi might have died of natural causes such as a heart attack or stroke.

The geneticists compared Ötzi's DNA with that of modern Europeans. Ötzi's mitochondrial DNA, passed down generation by generation on his mother's side, showed that her family line has disappeared.

Ötzi's paternal DNA told a different story. Ötzi's father's family, which migrated to Europe from the Near East about 6000 BCE, is alive and well and living in . . . Sardinia.

Sardinia is Italy's second-largest island. Apparently, island living—literally insular—has left Ötzi's modern family quite the same, DNA-wise, since Ötzi trekked the Alps.

A FRESH TAKE WITH A PLASTIC FAKE

When the experts looked back on their invasive search into Ötzi's corpse, they knew they needed a way to study Ötzi without defrosting him. They decided to copy the Iceman. A mummy dummy would solve lots of problems. It could be used numerous ways for research. And it could get on a plane and go on exhibit anywhere on earth.

Three-dimensional printing helped them out. The data from Ötzi's thousands of CAT scans was digitally

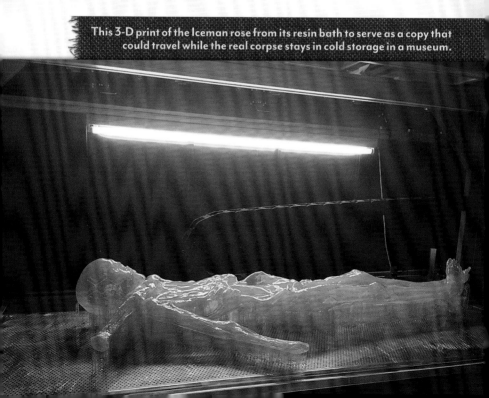

This 3-D print of the Iceman rose from its resin bath to serve as a copy that could travel while the real corpse stays in cold storage in a museum.

remixed to build a 3-D copy as a computer directed dozens of lasers to dance across a vat of liquid chemicals. When the lasers had done their work, an exact copy of Ötzi rose from the bath.

The artist and his team applied clay to the cast and texturized it to look like skin. They also sculpted details of "pathologies and damages," odd stuff on Ötzi's skin. Where the jackhammer had blown out Ötzi's hip, the team attached tendons made of fiber.

When it came time to give Ötzi his final coat of paint, the artist used new photos of Ötzi that captured him in the full spectrum of light: ultraviolet, visible, and infrared. Computer software translated the images into black-and-white to enhance every detail of his skin. Astonishingly, a hidden feature appeared, like a ghost caught on film. It was a tattoo, four more ink-blue lines on Ötzi's lower right chest.

Far back in human history, folks with aching joints were tattooed where it hurt. Practitioners of this art pierced the skin with thorns and then rubbed in campfire ashes. Carbon in the ash left its telltale blue.

Most of Ötzi's fifty-eight tattoos were inked near his joints—back, knees, and hands. But the ink on Ötzi's chest lay far from any joint. Ötzi's last autopsy had revealed stones in his gallbladder, heart disease, and parasitic whipworms in his bowels. Any or all probably hurt the Iceman. Did those four inky lines help relieve his pain?

Ötzi's geometric tattoos were the oldest ever discovered—until 2018, when scientists reported that a pair of mummies, one male and one female, turned up in Egypt sporting *figurative* tattoos. The male's were of a wild bull and a sheep, and the female's were S-shaped. These mummies dated back to Egypt's Predynastic days sometime between 4000–3100 BCE. Like Ötzi's folks, very ancient Egyptians inked their bodies.

NOW IT'S YOUR TURN...

Archaeologists, biologists, botanists, and geneticists pondered the evidence surrounding Ötzi's last hours:

- He'd been on the move—up on the mountain, then down in the valley, back up on the mountain, and finally, up to the glacier, where he died.
- He'd eaten a big meal, apparently in a sheltered place where he could rest and enjoy it.
- There was blood on his clothes, and not all of it was Ötzi's.
- He'd been shot in the back with an arrow, and he had begun to bleed out. But the arrow shaft had been removed.
- A blow to his head had made his brain hemorrhage. He fell after he was shot or someone hit him on the head to finish him off. Either way, his killer had turned him face down to get to the arrow shaft.

And then there was that beautiful ax, so expertly crafted from copper and wood. An ax that would be worth someone's time to take home. But no one had.

The experts think they have a good handle on Ötzi's curious tale. Just like an author of a good murder mystery, they ask key questions: Who? What? When? Where? Why? How?

Even so, as time moves on, experts can be proven wrong. You've read about that here.

Care to venture a guess? What do you think happened to Ötzi?

Ötzi researchers are still hot on the info trail. "Freezing to death is quite likely the main cause of death in this classic cold case," said Frank Rühli from the University of Zurich in Switzerland in 2017. His team declared that Ötzi damaged his skull after falling, protected though it was by his fur hat.

The original Ötzi lies in repose in the South Tyrol Museum of Archaeology. His plastic twin is on display in the United States, standing tall at the Dolan DNA Learning Center in Cold Spring Harbor, New York. Kids who visit are quick to point out that Ötzi looks like he's dabbing, and they connect by striking his pose.

FACTLET

WE BREAK DOWN ANCIENT HUMAN
HISTORY INTO SEVERAL "AGES."

THE STONE AGE began about three million years ago, long before *Homo sapiens* (that's us) appeared. During this stretch of time, prehumans and our ancestors made and used stone tools. Archaeologists now envision the Stone Age in three parts, old (Paleolithic), middle (Mesolithic), and new (Neolithic). About 3000 BCE, the Stone Age began to give way to . . .

THE BRONZE AGE, which arose when humans began to make metal tools of copper, or of an alloy of copper and tin called bronze. The Bronze Age began about five thousand years ago, although some scholars call its first thousand years the Copper Age. Not all cultures moved from stone to metal tools at the same time. China and Greece entered the Bronze Age around 5000 BCE, but in Britian, metal toolmaking didn't appear until 1900 BCE. A few isolated groups today live in Stone-Age ways.

THE IRON AGE arrived when people began to smelt iron from iron ore. Far stronger than bronze, iron was plentiful and became the metal of choice for tools and weapons. Iron transformed human life, beginning in the Middle East and southeastern Europe about 1200 BCE and about 600 BCE in China.

FACTLET

IN 2006, HELMUT SIMON died in a hiking accident in the Alps. His body was never recovered. Some could not help but ask if this was another example of the mummy's curse.

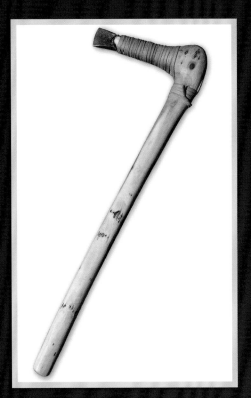

A German archaeological craftsman, Wulf Hein, made a copy of Ötzi's splendid copper ax.

CHAPTER FOUR

BOGGY BODIES IN TANNING BEDS

IN 1983, AN ENGLISHMAN NAMED ANDY MOULD WAS AT work in a mill, loading clumps of peat on a conveyor belt. He was making sure that logs or stumps didn't find their way into the whirling blades that shredded the peat so it could be bagged and sent to garden stores. He saw a suspicious lump, grabbed it, and tossed it to a coworker. As it hit the other guy's hands, debris went flying. This was no lump. It was part of a human head.

Andy Mould had found a bog body, a lifelike corpse that had spent hundreds or even thousands of years buried in a peat bog.

The next year, Andy, who was very good at his job, tossed a piece of wood off the conveyor. Again, the damp material flew off the log, and this time, a human leg lay there. The county archaeologist got the call and headed to the bog, a desolate place called Lindow Moss.

Thinking backward, he traced the leg's origins to its original location where he saw "a flap of dark, tanned skin projecting from below." There he found what the cutting machine hadn't destroyed, the top half of a man. The bottom half, presumably, was already shredded, bagged, and on its way to enrich the soil in someone's flower bed. (Some lower-body fragments, assumed to be from Lindow Man, turned up later.)

The bog body found its way to a museum in Manchester in northern England. For a time, its keepers called the corpse Pete Marsh. But soon enough, the body was removed to the British Museum in London. The science community gave the mummy a more dignified title: Lindow Man.

Whether Pete Marsh or Lindow Man, what made this Iron Age fellow a bog body was precisely what makes bogs bogs. A bog is a wetland, like marshes, fens, and swamps. In the Northern Hemisphere, bogs are found in Far North climates in Canada, Russia, and northern Europe and the British Isles.

Bogs are eerie spots, huge spongy masses of wet, dead plants. Often they arose from ancient glacial lakes over hundreds or thousands of years. These lakes didn't drain well, and as plants lived and died, they piled up in layers in the cold waters of the North.

There was little or no oxygen in the water, so bacteria couldn't do their usual job of decomposing the dead plants. Sphagnum moss grew like crazy and spread into thick mats across these lakes, thriving in these acidic conditions and driving acid levels even higher.

Year by year, the cycle continued, until bogs actually rose in domed shapes above water. Underneath, gravity did its

Both luck and cleverness led to Lindow Man's discovery in England in 1983.

thing, packing dead plant material into a thick, spongy mass we call peat or peat moss.

Bogs smell fresh, peaty, and of heather, a wild northern shrub with dangly purple flowers. "This is going to sound daft," explained an Irishman, "but they also smell of 'time.'"

For thousands of years, folks who lived in boggy places cut peat, dried it, and burned it for warmth and to cook. People so closely linked moss with bogs that they took to calling bogs "mosses."

SACRIFICE OR NOT?

Lindow Man is one among scores of bog mummies cut from bogs in northwestern Europe. A few centuries back, when people didn't know any better, bog bodies showed up, were admired, and were either reburied or fell apart in the oxygen-rich air and light of day.

Legends about bog bodies flourish. Murderers plunged their victims into bogs. Hapless men who had too much to drink had fallen in and drowned—most likely in spring when bogs are at their soggiest. Everyone knew how bogs were creepy and home to fairies, bog sprites, and a folk character named Will-o'-the-Wisp, a spooky sort of flame-like spirit.

In our day, UFOs have hovered over bogs—or were the frightened folks who called the cops merely seeing swamp gas burning on moonless nights?

Nevertheless, as people began to view the past with scientific eyes, they realized that bog mummies existed because:

- They'd been bogged quickly after death.
- Their semiwatery graves were acidic.
- The water was very cold.
- The bogs were anaerobic—no bacteria allowed.

Acidic conditions plus no bacteria means no body breakdown.

"The bog mummies are only preserved in so-called raised bogs. The sphagnum mosses there create an environment that has the ability to preserve collagen and keratin [in their tissue]," explained Ole Nielsen, director of the Museum Silkeborg in Denmark.

Scholars marveled at bog bodies. Plenty of skeletons were yanked from bogs all the time, but bog mummies were remarkable.

Sometimes the dank graves were so acidic that bog-body bones decalcified—dissolved. Even then, skin on these corpses stayed intact, though it turned a sort of shiny silvery brown. Wrinkles and hair, toenails and fingertips—these often stayed perfectly preserved in raised bogs, which could pile up eleven feet (3.4 meters) high.

Why was he there, this Lindow Man? Forty years ago, archeologists suggested that he'd been killed in a ritual execution. Some believe that his skull appears to have been bashed with hard blows that pushed bits of bone into his cranium. Not only that—he may have been garroted (strangled). And yet another possible insult: a slit throat.

"But not all of these injuries are certain," said Julia Farley, curator at the British Museum, who first laid eyes on Lindow Man when she was a child. "Both the garrote (which may be a necklace) and the slit throat (which could have been caused during decomposition) are conjectural."

Lindow Man looked about twenty-five years old. He had a sheared beard and moustache, smooth hands, and trimmed fingernails. His stomach contents revealed a small last meal of some kind of burned bread and mistletoe pollen, of all things. Mistletoe, the very plant used to promote holiday cheer! But it seemed this poor fellow hadn't gone looking for love.

"We don't know what Lindow Man's people would have called themselves, but he lived at a time when a family of languages and art styles was widely shared across Britain, Ireland, and much of Western Europe. Today we call the people who spoke these languages and made this art 'Celts,'" Farley noted.

Celts were the folks whose ancient beliefs brought us Halloween.

Celts believed that marshes and other wetlands were holy places where their gods hung out. Celtic priests, the druids, stood at the top of their social ladder. Radiocarbon dating showed that Lindow Man lived in the first century CE. Some who studied the druids took one look at Lindow Man and declared that he could have been a human sacrifice.

The burned bread and mistletoe fit nicely into passages from old folk tales. Bits of bread were handed out to a group of people. The one with the burned piece won the honor of becoming the next victim.

But were these stories true?

In the 1980s, after Lindow Man appeared, several scholars claimed that he had died at the hands of the druids. His possible three-way execution, unique last meal, and burial in a bog convinced them that their ideas were dead on. Wrote Anne Ross, an archaeologist, "Here we noted more of the forensic evidence: Not only did Lindow Man have a physique ideally suited to surviving druidic ordeals, but his body was remarkably unblemished. An unblemished body would be the mark of the sacrificial victim."

Not so fast, wrote another professor, Dr. Ronald Hutton. He'd built his career debunking theories about druids and witches and Celts and the like. He pointed out that there were a mere four grains of mistletoe pollen in Lindow Man's stomach. That, plus the probability that Lindow Man died in the days of Roman Britain. Where Rome ran things, human sacrifice was against the law.

Professors adore quarrels like these. "I think today almost everyone in the field would agree that the human sacrifice idea is far from proven and that it's very dubious to draw the druids into it!" added Farley.

In the meantime, there was a bog body to preserve. First, Lindow Man's keepers dunked him in a chemical bath to keep him from drying out and to help preserve his body. Next, they enfolded him in plastic wrap and placed him in a freezer, where he dried out. With the water in his tissues gone, Lindow Man would no longer decay and could go on display, and he did, at the British Museum.

But folks back home near Lindow Moss complained that the bog man belonged in a museum in nearby Manchester. Three times since, the Manchester Museum has welcomed its homeboy on loan, but his permanent residence is in London.

THE GRAVE MATTER OF GRAUBALLE MAN

A top candidate for Best in Show is a bog body discovered in 1952 in the Nebelgaard *mose* near the town of Grauballe, Denmark. (Danes call bogs *mose* in the same way the English call bogs *mosses*.)

A peat cutter stuck his spade in the bog and hit something. He turned up a cadaver, its throat slit. Word seeped out via the local postman, who told the doctor, who called experts, who called Professor P. V. Glob at of the National Museum of Denmark. And so the story of Grauballe Man unfolded.

Grauballe Man was X-rayed, his liver removed and sent to a laboratory for carbon dating. Fifties-style radiology studies reported he had a fractured skull and broken left leg. His bones looked like glass on the X-ray plates, because acid in the bog had decalcified them. The bog also turned his hair ginger-red.

Tests on his liver hinted that he'd died sometime in the third century BCE. It didn't seem a stretch for some scholars to think that Grauballe Man could have been an executed criminal.

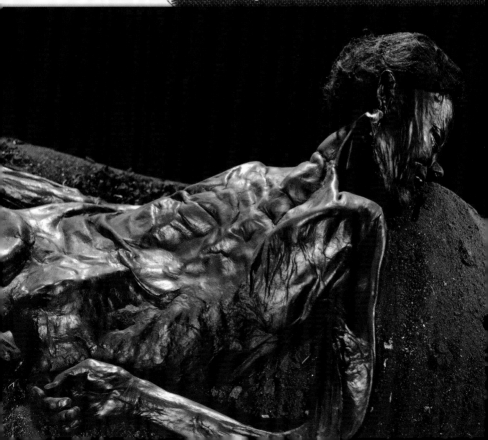

Over the years, new technology helps scientists learn new things about mummies like Grauballe Man.

These experts faced a fresh challenge. How could they preserve Grauballe Man now that he was aboveground? They had little experience to go on. In the 1800s, a German bog body had been smoked and dried like a piece of meat. This time, the Danes bathed their bog man in an oak-bark solution for a time, wiped him down, soaked him in oil and water, and plumped him up with body products like glycerin, lanolin, and cod liver oil.

Years later, better technology got the Danes rethinking Grauballe Man's story. Computed tomography rolled in about thirty years after the first tests, and Grauballe Man was duly scanned. His CAT scans changed minds when his keepers saw tiny details that they couldn't see in 1952, such as his last meal of mixed-grain porridge. His dreadful teeth, worn from chewing grit and coarse food, showed he'd been underfed as a child.

The body had been tampered with. Back in the 1950s conservators had remolded the body—unthinkable today. The new scans showed plenty of fake stuff in Grauballe Man, possibly to make him fit for public eyes. "We found things like blackboard rubbers [erasers] stuffed inside his thorax, and layers of putty under the skin on his face," said Niels Lynnerup, an anthropologist at the University of Copenhagen in Denmark. "You would never dream of doing this to an archaeological specimen now."

The CAT scans showed something else. Grauballe Man's cracked skull was not the work of a human after all.

The culprit was Mother Nature. Since about 300 BCE, Grauballe Man had lain in his grave as the bog piled on top of him. Some kind of pressure, that was, because the bog's weight had broken his skull and leg. It hadn't helped when a boy wearing wooden clogs stepped on his head as the poor soul was lifted from his peaty tomb.

So who was he, this Iron Age male? Was he a criminal? A prisoner of war? An object of sacrifice? With no ceremony, his body had been tossed into a waiting hole, dug perhaps, for its peat or for iron ore to make tools. What words were spoken over him, if there were words, went with him. Grauballe Man's people didn't leave written records about such things.

TELLING TALES OF TOLLUND MAN

If Grauballe Man is the poster boy for bog bodies, then another corpse is their grand old man. Two more Danish peat cutters had the shock of their lives when they unearthed a bog body in May 1950. Thinking they had a murdered man on their hands, they went to the police. In turn, the police dialed a museum, and before long, Professor Glob was at the bog to see the corpse himself.

The body was in an Iron Age peat pit. The dead man lay on his side as though asleep. His whiskered face and wrinkled brow made him look older than Grauballe Man. He was naked except for a leather belt and peaked sheepskin cap. Around his neck wound a double-stranded leather cord.

The autopsy examiner declared that the victim had been hanged—though it was odd that the vertebrae in his neck hadn't broken.

Laying eyes on such a lifelike creature left everyone stunned. Professor Glob felt as though the dead man's soul had "for a moment returned from another world, through a gate in the western sky."

It's thought that Glob named the body Tollund Man. As the years moved on, the bog man was tested with the latest in forensics: autopsied, fingerprinted, X-rayed, and CAT scanned. His first exam was conducted as though he had been a murder victim. He measured about five feet four inches (1.6 meters) tall. His feet were much too big for the rest of him, possibly because the body had shrunk in its boggy grave.

The examiner removed Tollund Man's stomach and intestines. He had pinworms in his bowels, signs that he and his people didn't wash their hands after toileting. The man's last supper had been sparse—plants and seeds and no meat. Was this because it was winter, or because he was being punished for a crime?

Most of Tollund Man's arms and fingers had skeletonized in the bog, becoming nothing but bone that looked like long claws. But the left thumb had not, and the police used it to create an ancient fingerprint. His feet and the thumb were plunked into a preserving fluid that kept them looking full and fresh, for a bog body.

Tollund Man's multiple injuries added to the mystery of why men and women were buried in bogs.

When the initial autopsy was complete, Tollund Man's head was cut away. His attendants did not try to preserve his decayed body, and besides, they didn't know how. His head, however, was a keeper, and they came up with a multistep plan to preserve it. In the final stage, "all water in the tissue of the head was gradually replaced with different types of wax; and as a result, it was possible to preserve the head with the features intact," said Nielsen.

Tollund Man's body was recreated in 1987 and attached to his real head. He went on permanent display in the Silkeborg Museum. The grand old man of bog bodies became a hero in books and poetry.

In 2015, researchers tried but failed to extract DNA from his femur. (They'll try again.) In 2017, 1.6-inch strands of hair were plucked from Tollund Man's skull to look for a chemical timeline of his travels. "The four-centimeter-long hair suggested that he had been in the local area the last four months of his life," Nielsen explained.

"A brand-new Carbon-14 dating in 2017 suggests that he died between 405 and 384 BCE. This is a very accurate dating—almost unheard off—and it proves him to have been living at the times of Socrates."

(If you haven't studied Socrates and ancient Greek history, you will!)

THE SORRY SAGA OF YDE GIRL

In 1897, peat cutters were at work in a bog near the Dutch town of Yde [EE-duh] when they chunked up a bog body. They took fright at the sight and ran for help. The body, a woman's, was covered by a shabby cloak. Half her long

Tollund Man's whiskers survived two thousand four hundred years in a Danish bog.

blond hair had been shaved. She'd been choked, some said, by her own woolen belt, which was wrapped around her neck. Her head and upper body were preserved, as were her feet. There wasn't anything else. "The reason was that her body was found in the course of peat dredging . . . underwater," said Vincent van Vilsteren, an archaeologist at the Drents Museum in the Netherlands. "The peat cutters tried to find as many parts as possible but missed quite some. So it was not a proper excavation."

The locals knew they had a prized discovery, but that didn't keep them from pulling most of her teeth and some hair to keep as souvenirs. Once the town mayor reached out to a museum of history and antiquities, the body was rescued and moved. The museum's president decided that an ape had been flung into that bog. Others disagreed. In any case, the woman/ape was thought to be about six hundred years old.

Time, of course, told a different tale. Yde Girl, as she was christened, was studied over the years. In 1988, her tissue was carbon dated, and she was declared about two thousand years old. She'd been executed, it seems, sometime between 54 BCE and 128 CE, during the heyday of the Roman Empire.

She was just sixteen years old, with a warped tale. She'd had scoliosis, curvature of her spine. Further exams revealed she'd been knifed near her collarbone even as she'd been strangled. Some wondered if Yde Girl had been sacrificed.

But others had a different notion. Half the girl's hair had been cut to the scalp, the other half left long. Perhaps the girl from Yde had been foolish and fallen in love with a married man. She had broken a rule in her society and paid the price by losing half her hair.

No record exists of how Yde Girl's first keepers kept her from rotting. In 1897, no one knew how to preserve bog bodies. Apparently, she dried out "rather like a dead cat that had been lying in the attic or a barn for about 100 years," van Vilsteren said. "Hard, dried out, and stiff—if you try to bend her skin, it will break off."

Early in the 2000s, Yde Girl toured museums in Europe, Canada, and the United States. She had companions on exhibit, too. One was Red Franz, a German mummy with a mop of blond hair turned red by the bog.

The others were the Weerdinge Couple, a pair found buried together in 1904 in the Netherlands. They were long thought to be a man and woman until someone noticed stubble on the smaller one's chin and realized that he was male, too.

The tour opened in Europe, and curious visitors crowded museums to view the bog dead and artifacts that fleshed out their daily lives. But when the exhibit opened in Canada, controversy awaited. Some museum employees, who were of First Nations (Native American) families, balked at putting the bog bodies on public display.

Yde Girl and an artist's model of her face have traveled the world.

For quite some time, Native people in the Americas had demanded that museums return skeletons and other remains of their peoples so they could be reburied in their home-lands. The First Nations employees didn't want to display the mummies. Putting dead people on exhibit—Native or European—disrespected their ancient ways.

The argument was settled when everyone gathered for a smudging ceremony. The First Nations folks burned fragrant herbs and asked the spirits to forgive any mistakes made as the exhibit came together. The ceremony also honored the souls of Yde Girl, Red Franz, and the Weerdinge

Couple before they settled into their display cases. At night, everything was covered in respect of the dead.

Yde Girl now rests at the Drents Museum. She wears a brown blanket and the pieces of her mantle. In keeping with the way things are done in Europe, Yde Girl and her fellow boggers are uncovered, night and day.

WE THREE KINGS OF IRELAND ARE . . .

Early in our millennium, bodies popped up in Ireland's bogs. In 2003, a pair of corpses appeared, not far from each other. One was short, and the other was a giant, though all the bog could offer were his torso and arms.

The short fellow, Clonycavan Man, from County Meath, had only his head, trunk, and upper arms to show for his time in the bog that had tanned him into leather. Apparently, the peat-cutting machine had destroyed the rest of him. He lived sometime between 392 BCE and 201 BCE. He'd died young—not yet twenty-five.

He'd met a gruesome end—three ax gashes in his skull and one more in his chest, nose broken, stomach ripped wide open. He wore his hair cut close in back, but the top he'd grown very long and he'd used pine resin to comb it into a sort of Mohawk. Tests on his hair showed he'd been eating fruits and veggies—he'd died later in summer as the crops came in.

The big man appeared to have been six feet four inches (two meters) tall. They tagged him Old Croghan [KROCK-un] Man, because he was found at Old Croghan, County Offaly, in Ireland's midsection. The archaeologists who rushed to meet him were impressed with the size and power of his arms. He'd walked the earth sometime between 362 BCE and 175 BCE and died in his early twenties. He'd been a regular meat eater, as tests on his hair and nails showed, but his final feast had been grains and buttermilk.

Old Croghan Man's hand

Old Croghan Man's killers had cut holes in his arms and run spancels, animal restraints, through them. (In his day,

Old Croghan Man's peculiar injuries led to all kinds of guessing about why he died.

spancels kept cows from moving as they were milked or from running off during cattle raids.) He'd been stabbed and, finally, cut in two.

Both were found along age-old borders that marked Irish kingdoms. Forty bog bodies have appeared in spots along these ancient boundaries.

Old Croghan Man and his short neighbor shared a bizarre detail. Their nipples had been cut through. This startling mutilation got archaeologists thinking. Had these men been kings in Ireland? The cut nipples and multiple wounds provided clues.

"The killings tend to be excessive," said Eamonn P. Kelly, a curator at the National Museum of Ireland. "More is done to the bodies than would be required to bring about their deaths. Bog bodies may have their throats cut, been stabbed in the heart, and have other cut marks. However, it is absolutely not torture, but a form of ritual sacrifice."

Kelly felt sure that both men had been kings, kings sacrificed to their Celtic gods. The Celts, it seems, practiced an odd show of loyalty to their leaders. In some kind of ceremony, the ruled sucked their rulers' nipples.

Mutilated nipples = no king. For whatever reason, these unlucky rulers had lost their game of thrones. There was a host of reasons to think why, including the ways Celts worshipped. In the Celtic religion, the king represented the sun god and was symbolically married to the Goddess, the Creator of all living things.

Thanks to this mystical marriage, an Irish king had a sacred duty to the land, and to its people and animals, as well. If life was good, he got the cred. But when the harvest was poor? Blame the king, cut his nipples, and sacrifice him to the Goddess. "The Goddess had a threefold nature," Kelly explained, "as goddess of fertility, or sovereignty, and/or death or war. This is why kings were killed by the ritual threefold method whereby a variety of injuries were inflicted, including blunt trauma, stabbing, and drowning by immersion in bog water."

Other scholars sneer at the notion that the Celts and other northern Europeans worshipped a goddess in the first place. Those quarrels go on.

"I see these bodies as ambassadors who have come down to us from a former time with a story to tell," Kelly said. "And even though it was thousands of years ago, it is still in each and every case a human tragedy."

Another bog man showed up in 2011. His chest didn't survive the milling machine that turned him up.

No Iron Age fellow was he. This guy, christened Cashel Man after Cashel bog in County Laois [LEESH], was twice as old as the others: a Bronze Age man who lived four thousand years ago. He is the oldest fleshed bog person ever found.

Finding Cashel Man was remarkable. Why? Archaeologists have discovered that the earliest Irish, who lived in the Stone Age, burned their dead. We call this cremation. When we bury the dead, that's inhumation.

Cremation was routine for Ireland's dead through the Bronze Age and into the Celtic Iron Age. The Celts seemed to believe that fire released the soul from the body.

Another piece of evidence at the burial site added to the chatter. Cashel Man, like Old Croghan Man, had been

dumped in a bog on the boundary of royal lands that surrounded sacred hills where local kings were "inaugurated," Kelly explained. Clonycavan Man lay on the territorial boundary between two ancient kingdoms. "Boundaries were perceived of as portals to the otherworld" with strong ritual meaning.

Cashel Man is the oldest fleshed bog person ever found.

FACTLET

———— ◆ ————

IN 2016, AN IRISHMAN cutting peat from a bog in County Meath unearthed a twenty-two-and-a half-pound (ten kilo) chunk of . . . butter! The waxy discovery smelled like strong cheese and, according to the experts, was still edible, which is incredible, considering it's about two thousand years old. Noted Kelly: "Bog butter is a common offering found in boundary bogs and was associated with seeking protection of the cattle herds and a good yield of dairy produce."

FACTLET

———— ◆ ————

MAN BUNS ARE NOTHING NEW. Just the head of the now-named Osterby Man was found wrapped in deerskin in Germany in 1948. His hair—turned red from lying in a bog for two thousand years—was wound in a fancy knot on one side of his head. The Roman historian Tacitus had written about these updos worn by a Germanic tribe, the Suebi.

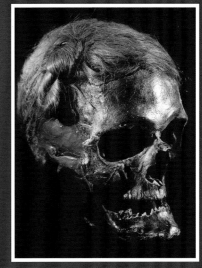

Osterby Man

CHAPTER FIVE

ARM TATTOO IN INKY BLUE: THE ALTAI PRINCESS

SOMETIME AROUND 400 BCE, LIKELY IN THE MONTH OF June, a funeral took place on the high ground of Eastern Central Asia. Grieving people buried a favored daughter in their sacred pasture on the Ukok Plateau. This harsh land stood in plain view of the Altai Mountains, a twelve-hundred-mile range of peaks that reaches from the Gobi Desert northwest through China, Mongolia, Russia, and Kazakhstan.

It's possible that this woman, who was between twenty-eight and thirty, had died miles away from this hallowed ground. But her nomadic people, the Pazyryks, wished to bury her in exactly the right spot. Here, they spent their winters, when heavy winds blew snow from the grass, offering a spot for their sheep and horses to feed. Here, the Pazyryks buried their dead. Today, twenty-five hundred years on, these are still called the Pastures of Heaven. They lie in the Altay Republic in Siberia, Russia.

Even in summer, the Ukok Plateau, a full mile and a half above sea level, is a chilly place with icy ground. The Pazyryks dug a burial chamber nearly ten feet (three meters) deep—as far as they could into the icy ground. The chamber, its footprint about the size of a small storage shed, was lined with logs so that it felt like a home.

Inside, they placed grave goods, such as thick felt rugs and drinking vessels of ceramic, wood, and animal horn. They also set dishes of mutton on short-legged tables. During her life, the young woman would have taken the tables apart and brought them with her as she moved. During her afterlife, those tables would stay set for dinner.

Loving hands began the careful task of embalming the young woman, head to toe. They shaved her head and trepanned her skull, cutting a hole in back. Brains rot quickly when someone dies, so the embalmers extracted hers and replaced it with vegetable matter. Her eyeballs, also apt to rot fast, were replaced with fur.

The embalmers removed her internal organs and filled the body cavity with peat and bark. Their tannins would seep into her soft tissues to help preserve them. Her spine was cut in two spots, to allow her body to bend. Finally, she was stitched back up with thread made from horses' manes and tails.

They dressed the young woman in her best. Her knee-length blouse was spun of wild silk from some far-off land and trimmed in maroon. Her red-and-white woolen skirt was decorated with a tasseled belt. Thigh-high boots completed her outfit. Atop her shaved head, she wore a wig and a very tall hat adorned with wooden birds and a griffin, a lion with an eagle's head, wings, and talons. Her necklace was strung with wood-carved snow leopards covered in thin sheets of gold. (When the mummy was discovered, it took the experts a while to decide that these were felines and not camels, as some had reported at first.)

After she was dressed, the undertakers placed her body on a felt pad in a coffin carved out of a larch-wood log. Thanks to those cuts in her spine, she could lie in a curve on her side with her face to the east, as though curling up to sleep. A wooden lid was fixed on top of her coffin, and bronze nails were driven into it to keep it closed forever.

The young woman had her pick of mounts to ride. Six horses, bridled and saddled in wool felt, were slaughtered next to the grave. The dead animals, front legs extended

outward and rear legs tucked in, were eased into the pit along the burial chamber's north wall.

Once all was ready for the young woman's trip to the sacred pastures, a lid of logs was dropped on top of the burial chamber, a roof for her little cabin in the ground.

Two others were buried on top of her chamber. One, a man, was gravely disabled, with deformed legs and spine. His misshapen body went into an ordinary casket of wood and stone, and this was plunked directly on top of the woman's burial chamber. Three more sacrificed horses went with him into his grave. At some point, bone fragments from a younger person found their way into that spot, as well.

They filled the hole with soil and rock, and then more hands worked to build a mound of rocks and boulders on top. Centuries later, people named this structure a *kurgan*, a Russian word with Turkish roots meaning "fortress."

Eventually the Pazyryks passed out of history. Another group of people took over, and the Pazyryks' pile of rocks told grave robbers exactly where to dig. Looking for gold and jewels, they dug into the topmost grave, disturbing the misshapen bones of the man buried there. But underneath, the log burial chamber and larch-wood coffin stayed hidden.

Water began to seep into the burial chamber. In this high-altitude cold, it froze quickly, and a coat of ice, an ice lens as it's called, formed on top of the tomb. Now frozen in time, the young woman could rest in peace.

HISTORY, HORSES, AND HERODOTUS

The Pazyryk people didn't read or write their language, so they had no way of keeping a record of the young woman's grave. When the Pazyryks died off, only the earthly objects they buried in thousands of graves could tell future people about their horse-centered way of life.

In faraway Greece, however, a historian named Herodotus *did* write down thrilling tales of horse-riding peoples as he traveled the known world of his time. Herodotus, who lived from about 484 BCE to 429 BCE, covered great distances. He visited Egypt and the Middle East. From

Greece, he journeyed north to the Danube River and east along the north shore of the Black Sea.

In one book, he described the Scythians, who lived near the Black Sea. The Scythians, a seminomadic people, ruled on horseback. They controlled their part of the world from about 1000 BCE to 200 BCE. Centuries later, archaeologists harnessed their name to the variety of horse-riding peoples who lived across Eurasia. Experts who studied the Pazyryks decided that many of their customs and beliefs mirrored the Scythians.

The highest-ranking members of these horse-riding peoples, kings and chieftains and the like, merited all kinds of extra attention in the hereafter. Herodotus reported these spine-chilling tales about Scythian burials to his Greek-reading audience:

> Here, when the king dies, they dig a grave,
> which is square in shape, and of great size.
> When it is ready, they take the king's corpse,
> and, having opened the belly, and cleaned out
> the inside, fill the cavity with a preparation
> of chopped cypress, frankincense, parsley-
> seed, and anise-seed . . . and, placing it on a
> wagon, carry it about through all the different
> tribes . . . On completing the circuit of all . . .
> they come to the tombs of the kings.

Fixated on the Scythians, Herodotus wrote more:

> There the body of the dead king is laid in the grave ... In the open space around the body of the king they bury one of his concubines, first killing her by strangling, and also his cupbearer, his cook, his groom, his lacquey [lackey, servant], his messenger, some of his horses, firstlings of all his other possessions, and some golden cups; for they use neither silver nor brass. After this they set to work, and raise a vast mound above the grave.

The Scythians buried three kinds of grave goods with their dead. The first were horses, complete with saddles and bridles. The second were weapons of battle such as bows and arrows, axes, swords, and picks. Third in this Scythian triad were everyday objects decorated with fanciful horses twisted into S-shapes, or pairs of animals in fighting mode.

The Scythians depended on horses to preserve and protect their way of life. Their bodies provided meat; their hides, clothing. Mares supplied milk to make a drink called *kumis*. Horsehair from manes and tails became thread for sewing. The Scythians traded horses, rode them from place to place, and used them to pull wagons and carts. They also used horses to herd, explore new lands, and wage wars. Horses were so important to the nomads that they buried them in graves with the dead.

DID HERODOTUS HORSE AROUND?

As Herodotus's stories were passed around, his readers thought he was messing with the facts. The Greeks, who wore togas, could not easily imagine how people wore pants and took their dead kings on tour. Later scholars also believed that Herodotus had made up his Scythian tales. Like the Pazyryks, these Scythians had left no written records about their deeds or steeds. The truth behind Herodotus's histories was always in doubt—until archaeology arrived in the Altai.

In the 1900s, archaeologists began digging into graves all over Eurasia. Russian archaeologist Sergei Rudenko and a colleague headed to the Altai to excavate ancient burials. There, in 1947, they unearthed the region's very first mummies.

We don't know what these ancient folks called themselves, but Rudenko named them Pazyryks. What was more, the Russian archaeologist, after viewing the graves, suspected that Pazyryk customs were similar to Scythian ways. All three types of Scythian grave goods also appeared in Pazyryk burials. It seemed that Herodotus's histories weren't so far-fetched.

These mummies were studied to death and then found their new resting place in a museum in Leningrad. (Leningrad, now called St. Petersburg, has changed names over the years, but that's a lesson for a different book.)

In 1990, a new generation of Russian archaeologists came back to the Altay Republic explored by Rudenko decades before. Dr. Natalia Polosmak, the team leader, hailed from the Russian Institute of Archaeology and Ethnography in Novosibirsk, a town in Siberia.

She and her crew headed for the chilly Ukok Plateau, chomping on the bit to find Pazyryk kurgans.

The team took a five-hour chopper ride south from Novosibirsk and set up camp in a piece of no-man's-land between Russia and China. That first summer, the team dug up two skeletons, one of a male warrior and one of a woman who well might have been a warrior herself.

Two disappointing seasons followed. "In the deep, long winter of Novosibirsk, I sat with my books and my artifacts, wondering what the Pazyryk people had really been like. In my imagination, they were standing around me, their eyes imploring, 'Natasha, you have to tell about our lives. You must do it.'"

Then, in 1993, Polosmak returned yet again to the Ukok Plateau. Heavy snow forced her supply trucks to stop early, in sight of a mediocre-looking kurgan that showed every sign it had been robbed.

Something—those pictures in her head, perhaps—compelled Polosmak to dig there, just inside the barbed-wire border that marked no-man's-land between Russia and China.

It took two weeks to remove the rocks covering the kurgan. The team then dug down to uncover the same coffin the robbers had found: that misshapen man buried with three horses and the bone fragments of someone else. But what else lay in that kurgan? Could there be a burial chamber like the Pazyryks used? Polosmak held her breath as they cut through to the lid.

The team was in luck. To their great fortune, those grave robbers hadn't studied Pazyryk patterns. The larch-log lid, directly under the disturbed coffin, had stayed intact.

They pulled it away, revealing a burial chamber frozen in a solid chunk

This drawing shows the Altai Princess as she was discovered as well as her imagined burial clothing.

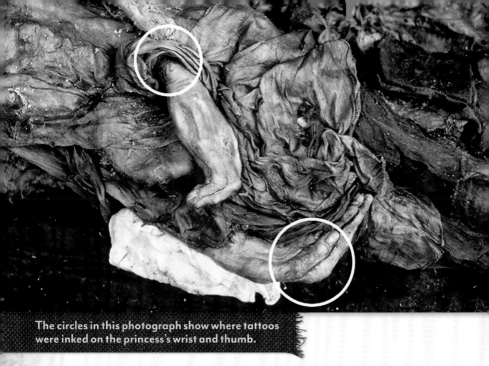

The circles in this photograph show where tattoos were inked on the princess's wrist and thumb.

of ice. The team heated lake water with blowtorches and began to bathe the ice block with warm water. The lid of a casket appeared, and then two small tables floated up when the chamber filled with water. A chunk of mutton still sat on one.

As they worked, the air filled with a strong smell from mutton and horseflesh. Along the chamber walls, the bodies of six horses lay in piles, still wearing their decorated bridles. Their skulls bore the marks of a battle-ax; they'd been slaughtered at the grave site and lowered into the chamber.

The team next removed the bronze coffin nails and lifted the lid. More melting with hot water in a tin cup slowly revealed a jawbone. Was it a skeleton? Next, they saw the flesh on a cheek. A mummy? Then they saw a shoulder covered in fur. Underneath was real human skin, with the deep midnight blue tattoo of a fanciful, griffinish beast.

Mummy!

Bit by bit, a Pazyryk mummy began to emerge. Polosmak sensed—and hoped—that it was a woman. The gold foil covering its jewelry had disintegrated into little pieces that sparkled from the bottom of the coffin. Fragrant coriander seeds lay in a dish next to a headdress. Liquid had pooled underneath the headdress—dye, perhaps. A pair of swans and more adorned it.

The mummy was a woman. Polosmak described her:

> In the crook of the lady's knee was a red cloth case containing a small hand mirror of polished metal with a deer carved into its back. Beads wound around her wrist, and more tattoos decorated her wrist and thumb. She was tall, about five feet six. She had doubtless been a good rider, and the horses in the grave were her own. As we worked, the fabric gradually revived around her limbs, softening the outline of her legs, the swell of her hip. And somehow, in that moment, the remains became a person. She lay sideways, like a sleeping child, with her long, strong, aristocratic hands crossed in front of her. Forgive me, I said to her.

The frozen woman took many names—Altai Princess, Ukok Princess, Siberian Ice Maiden. (Some simply called her "girl.") The mummy was hustled off the plateau by helicopter, which had to make a forced landing in an August snowstorm. Was it a mummy's curse? Even Polosmak mused about the situation. "I couldn't help but wonder how much meddling we had done to spiritual balance of the world above Ukok."

Unable to fly in bad weather, the mummy went by bus to a freezer at the institute. But the longer travel time caused microbes to darken the lady's delicate skin. She was rushed to Moscow, Russia's capital, where the embalmed body of Vladimir Lenin, a national hero, had been on display for years. The same experts who kept Lenin looking good worked their magic and preserved the lady, tattoos and all.

This deep-blue body art added to the intrigue of the Altai Princess. Picture this on her left shoulder:

A deer with . . .

   🌀 a griffin's beak,

   🌀 a goat's horns decorated with griffin heads,

   🌀 and another griffin's head on its back.

On her arm below the deer, a spotted panther stood ready to pounce, mouth open at the legs of a sheep. A deer head was inked on her wrist and another animal on her left thumb.

What did they all mean? No one was exactly sure.

The tattoos, lovely body art, were rife with symbols. They showed fights between predator and prey. There were earthly beasts and otherworldly animals as well. Here in this tomb, three or four time zones from where the Scythians had lived, was evidence of the Scythian triad: horses, weapons, and magical beasts. Clearly, the Pazyryk lifestyle was connected like links on their golden necklaces to other Eurasian groups and, finally, to those mysterious Scythians of Herodotus.

The magnificent horses, slaughtered and buried with the princess, added another curious detail. The researchers examined twigs in the animals' stomachs and horse botfly larvae in their bowels. Based on their knowledge of trees and insects, they decided something else: The princess had been buried in June.

A mythical beast was tattooed on the Altai Princess's shoulder. At right, an artist's drawing shows what the tattoo looks like.

A CHOSEN ONE

The tomb of a lone woman signaled her special standing among the Pazyryk people. She might have been a storyteller or a warrior. But fresh research pointed the experts in another direction. In 2014, more than twenty years after the Altai Princess was removed from her tomb, her MRI (magnetic resonance imaging) scan startled everyone who studied her.

The princess had been gravely ill. She'd had osteomyelitis, a bone infection. The scans also suggested that cancer had spread through her body. She could have suffered for years. Possibly the illness had weakened her so much she'd fallen from her horse; there were signs of damage to her right temple, hip, and knee.

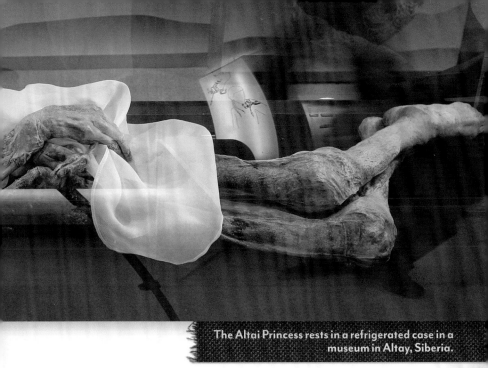

The Altai Princess rests in a refrigerated case in a museum in Altay, Siberia.

It's likely that the young woman inhaled the vapors of burning coriander seeds, the seeds buried with her, in order to relieve her pain. What was more, to her people, the suffering princess might well have served as a shaman, a holy person in touch with the spirit world. Perhaps the Pazyryks believed that the woman communicated with their dead who had ridden to heavenly pastures before her.

A BITTER BARGAIN

Many who lived in the Altai Princess's homeland objected to the woman's travels both for research and public exhibits. When the Altai land shook with earthquake tremors, people said the spirits were angry that the Altai Princess had been taken from her grave.

But the archaeologists who studied the Altai Princess explained that she was a Pazyryk, not the same ancestral line as the Altai land's Native peoples. "The soul is somewhere else and we're studying the remains," said Vyacheslav Molodin, Natalia Polosmak's husband, of the Siberian Branch of Russian Academy of Sciences. But to the locals, this opinion didn't matter. Among the Altai, respect for the spirit world runs deep.

The two sides reached an uneasy agreement. In 2012, the Altai Princess was moved to a new museum in Altay's capital built to house her remains. Her mummy lies in a glass sarcophagus, custom built and refrigerated. To protect her modesty, she wears a filmy veil over her torso. Still, the museum's curator wasn't quite sure that the princess should be on exhibit. There's still that tug between research, on the one hand, and spiritual beliefs, on the other.

The dispute goes on. The Altai pastures are now off-limits to archaeologists, set aside as a place of reverence and respect for the Altai people. But climate change has come to Siberia. With temperatures rising, the remaining burial chambers—and there are many—will likely melt. Once they defrost, they'll rot.

In the end, Mother Nature may have the last word in what happens to the Pazyryk graves.

FACTLET

A SCIENTIST WHO STUDIES insects revealed that the Altai Princess died in the second half of June. He based his decision on his knowledge of the life cycle of horse botflies, insects that have a peculiar link with equines. Horse botflies—there are three species—prey specifically on horses. They lay eggs as close as possible to a horse's mouth.

In this warm, moist environment, the eggs hatch into larvae, tiny maggots called *bots*. After a time, the horse swallows the bots, which then hook onto the lining of its stomach or intestines. The bots live inside the gut for about seven months moving through more stages of growth.

When the weather outside is just right, the bots detach and the horse poops them out. The mature larvae enter the soil below the dung pile and pupate. In two weeks to two months, depending on the season, they emerge as adults. Of course, these horse botflies need mates, and their best chance to find a date is in a pile of manure.

An adult horse botfly.

Horse botfly larvae live and mature inside a horse's stomach and intestines.

FACTLET

DID THE ANCIENTS such as the Greeks and Scythians think up griffins and other mythical beasts based on dinosaur fossils? American history detective Adrienne Mayor thought so. She put her ideas into a book. Some readers agree, but others say that her suggestion is fanciful.

Sometime between 500 and 400 BCE, a Scythian wore these golden plaques (PLAX) to decorate a piece of clothing. These ornaments feature an imaginary beast, the griffin.

CHAPTER SIX

SICK: MUMMY MEDICAL MYSTERIES

YOU DON'T HAVE TO GO BACK THOUSANDS OF YEARS TO find mummies. Lots of them are a mere two- or three hundred years old. That's modern, when you look at how long our species has been on the planet. *Homo sapiens*—that's us—appeared two hundred thousand years ago.

Modern mummies surprise and intrigue us as archeological finds. What's more, they often turn out to be gifts to the medical community. Their well-preserved bodies hold the secrets of diseases and deaths that still plague us.

THE FORGOTTEN MUMMIES OF VÁC

In Vác, Hungary, three hundred years ago, the Dominican church served its people throughout their lives. Babies were baptized, young couples were wed, and worshippers prayed. When a life ended, it was celebrated in a funeral in the church, as well.

For nearly one hundred years, from 1738 until 1831, many in Vác were laid to rest under the floor of their Roman Catholic church in its large, airy crypt. They and their families planned for their bodies to spend eternity there, close to the sacred relics of saints held in the church above them. There were all kinds of people in the crypt—babies in baby dresses, men in traditional tunics and pants, women in their dresses and caps. Holy people—nuns in their habits and monks in their robes—also rested there.

Not only did these dead wear their finest; their coffins were fancied up as well, personal touches included. Large pine-board coffins held the grownups' remains and were painted yellow, gray, or brown. Small coffins cradled the children, but these were painted blue or green.

Most coffins were embellished with bright designs and images of flowers, skulls, and other symbols of death and faith. A few bore images of Christ on the cross. Many were painted with lifelike skulls and crossbones, together with a grim reminder written in Latin: *Memento mori*—Remember you must die.

As life went on and newly dead were carried down the steps from the church to the crypt, the coffins were shoved aside, small ones piled on top of bigger ones. In time, entire families were crowded together. At some point, possibly, the crypt couldn't hold any more bodies, because a jumble of remains were stuffed into an ossuary, a large vessel specially designed to hold bones.

In the meantime, doctors grew wiser about how diseases passed from person to person. Possibly Vác officials realized that housing dead people under a church might not create the healthiest of environments for those above. The authorities closed the crypt and sealed its two points of entry. One, behind the altar, disappeared when the main church was renovated. The other, running downstairs from the bell tower, was eventually tiled over. Only a pair of air shafts that ran from outside into the crypt opened to the outside world.

Time went on, and the children of these dead and then their grandchildren passed on. Wars took place, and governments came and went. For more than one hundred fifty years, two hundred sixty-two coffins lay undisturbed under the church floor. No one remembered the souls who lay in their painted pine boxes.

Until one day in 1994. When the church was undergoing a major facelift, a construction worker looking around in the bell tower noticed that a tile wall could be covering something. He went knocking on the wall, and it made a hollow sound.

Once the crypt was reopened, it must have been quite a jolt for whoever opened all those hidden coffins. Instead of clothed skeletons, the pine boxes held clothed mummies, natural mummies—accidental, some might say. Shrunken, yet lifelike, many held crosses or rosaries in their hands.

Mother Nature had done her thing with air and something else. Winter, spring, summer, or fall, those two ventilation shafts had channeled cool, dry air into the crypt. The something else was pinesap, sticky and acidic, that had seeped from the pine boards. The undertakers had also sprinkled pine shavings inside the coffins to absorb liquid leaking from the corpses as they decomposed. With acid to kill bacteria and bugs, and plenty of air flowing by, the bodies had dried out. Easy queasy.

TRACING A TRAIL OF TUBERCULOSIS

Researchers jumped at the chance to study the lives of the people interred in the crypt. They pored over the church registers, ink-and-paper records of the living and dead who had passed through its doors for baptisms, confirmations, weddings, and funerals.

Linking the dead to these church records proved even easier in Vác, because many coffins displayed their owners' names. The researchers began to build family trees, and they learned that entire families had been laid to rest in the crypt. These cryptic clues led to more questions: Why did all these people die? Was there a link among their deaths?

Forensic experts studied many of the Vác mummies in their laboratories. When they analyzed the mummies' lung tissue, their results pointed to tuberculosis as the culprit. Tuberculosis is caused by a bacterium with a long Latin name, *Mycobacterium tuberculosis*. TB, as this disease has been called for years, is a natural born killer.

Tuberculosis has scourged humans for thousands of years. The disease spreads through droplets from the throats or lungs of infected people when they breathe, cough, or sing. A single cough can send three thousand infective droplets into the air, and as few as ten bacilli can cause an infection. Indeed, tuberculosis bacteria are tough, but the immune system of a healthy adult or child can either fight the disease or suppress it into an inactive form called latent TB.

If TB takes hold in a weaker person, however, the lungs fill with nodules, lumps of abnormal tissue or cheesy masses. Often TB patients cough up bright-red blood. There's a reason why TB was called consumption back in the day. The disease can literally consume the lungs and bones as it invades its victim. TB also can involve the brain, skin, eyes, digestive system, sex organs, kidneys, and bladder.

As testing on the Vác bodies moved forward, astonishing facts appeared. DNA from *M. tuberculosis* bacteria appeared among seven out of ten. But not everyone actually *had* TB. Some carried it in their bodies but never got sick. Others had TB but got well and died from something else. In fact, the average age of the mummies was about sixty, about ten years less than life expectancy today. The immune systems in older folks probably had built up resistance to the bacterium.

THE FAMILY ORLOVITS

Among the dead in the Vác crypt were three members of a family.

> **MICHAEL ORLOVITS**, a miller, grinder of wheat to make flour. Born in 1765. Died in 1806.

> **VERONICA SKRIPETZ**, Michael's wife. Born in 1770. Died in 1808.

> **JOHANNES ORLOVITS**, their third child. Born in 1800. Died in 1801.

In 2010, the little family went on exhibit with lots of other mummies across the United States. From time to time, one or more mummies were removed from museums to medical schools for checkups. In California, a wife-husband team of radiologists did CAT scans of Veronica and Johannes. Ever so gently, mother and baby were eased from their carrying cases onto X-ray equipment for scanning.

The images proved what the experts in Hungary had suspected all along. Veronica Skripetz was a petite woman whose small size hinted that she'd been sick for months. Veronica's CAT scans showed signs of scarring in her lungs, proof that TB had killed her. But she hadn't infected everyone around her.

Baby Johannes didn't seem to have TB. He was perfectly healthy with fat and chubby legs that healthy babies have. He showed no signs of tuberculosis. Something else had killed the little boy, and quickly. His CAT scan pointed to his intestines, which looked oddly empty. The radiologists decided that Johannes had died from dysentery, massive diarrhea from a deadly microbe in his gut.

Michael's scan took place at a different hospital and left the radiologists bewildered. They wondered if Michael had been autopsied after he died, because part of his breastbone

Veronica Skripetz, as well as her child and husband, were mummified in a wooden coffin under a church floor in Vác, Hungary.

Researchers wondered why a healthy-looking baby like Johannes Orlovits died.

and midsection were gone. The CAT scan also revealed a dislocated shoulder and a broken leg that had healed, leaving his left leg shorter than the right. Sometime after Michael died, someone had plunked in a wooden peg to attach his head to his body.

This evidence hinted that Michael had had an accident on the job. Millers worked around heavy grinding stones and running rivers, and danger lingered. Even later, DNA research couldn't find "conclusive evidence of TB" in Michael. He died from something else.

"It was a tragic life," said Ildikó Pap, the anthropologist who cared for Michael's mummy family at their museum home in Hungary. "They were too young to die."

"I don't think he would have liked to be put on display, but we are treating him with dignity."

The scan offered up another surprise. Between Michael's arm and back, someone had placed a metal crucifix of Jesus on the cross.

The Orlovits family counted as only three among many mummies of people and animals on exhibit with them. Visitors left written comments, including one that said, "One of the reasons

Michael Orlovits's CAT scan revealed possible on-the-job injuries.

I don't want to be a docter [*sic*]." But the Orlovits family humbled many of their visitors. As Papa, Mama, and baby, they spoke to visitors' hearts.

Said one of the family's caretakers: "They're not objects. They're not artifacts. They're people."

Today Michael, Veronica, and Johannes rest in the Hungarian Natural History Museum.

THE SOAP LADY OF PHILADELPHIA

In 1874, as the United States was about to celebrate the one-hundredth anniversary of the Declaration of Independence, the city of Philadelphia was on the move. Workmen cleared anything that stood in their way as new streets stretched out and buildings rose. But when a bunch of bodies showed up, they had to stop.

They'd come across an old burial ground. The unmarked graves held a muddle of bones, plus two very odd lookers, a woman and a man. These were obviously human remains, but they had morphed into waxy forms, looking for all the world like giant lumps of gray soap. The woman, her mouth agape, had no teeth and just strands of hair. The man had fared better: He was still wearing his knee-high stockings.

Dr. Joseph Leidy, a pioneer researcher in anatomy, was called. He decided to bring the odd couple in for further examinations. The trouble was, there was a law against such things, as the local grave keeper reminded him. Then the grave keeper, with a wink and a nod to the doctor, said, "I give the bodies up to the order of relatives."

Dr. Leidy took the hint and sent a wagon to pick up the bodies, along with a letter stating that the bodies were his very own grandparents. With sly humor, he named them Mr. and Mrs. *Ellenbogen*—German for elbow. As when you elbow someone kidding around, the doctor had poked fun at Philadelphia's old burial laws.

Dr. Leidy spent some time going over the bodies. He marveled at what had happened in the grave. Instead of decaying, the flesh had saponified—turned into a soap-like chemical compound called adipocere [a-di-po-SEER]. He decided that the Ellenbogens had died of yellow fever about 1792.

The doctor split up the couple and sent the woman's corpse to the Mütter Museum of the College of Physicians of Philadelphia. The male mummy eventually arrived at the Smithsonian Museum in Washington, DC.

The female mummy took the name Soap Lady and became a leading exhibit at the museum. "Old and probably ugly, with a nutcracker profile," her curator declared in 1947. But when he combed through old city records looking for the Soap Lady, he couldn't find anyone named Ellenbogen. Nor could he find that anyone had died of yellow fever in 1792. The pair of soap mummies were not Joseph Leidy's "Ellenbogen" grandparents.

In 1987, a new team took a clean look at the Soap Lady using a portable X-ray machine. They were surprised to see that, inside her waxen body, her bones were in good shape. They calculated that she'd been about forty when she died. It seemed odd that she was toothless. At forty, most people had at least some teeth—unless some dreaded condition had struck her at a young age.

The X-rays showed other evidence that piqued their interest. Buttons and straight pins had been found with the Soap Lady. Her undertaker would have fastened her shroud with the pins. He also pinned the lady's chinstrap tight to stop her jaw from dropping open. (It did so, anyway.)

These bits of forensic evidence further convinced the experts that Dr. Leidy had lied back in 1874. The Soap Lady couldn't have died in 1792. Her buttons weren't manufac-

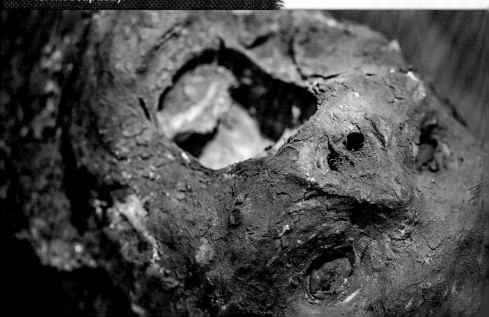

Scientists still seek the exact cause of death for the Soap Lady.

tured until the 1830s. Same with the straight pins; they had rounded heads. Pins from the 1790s would have bent at the top.

In 2007, the team returned with updated equipment to take more X-rays. They revised the Soap Lady's age downward by ten years. Still, the exam left many questions unanswered, including her cause of death.

More testing was in the Soap Lady's future. She was a tough study, because invasive tests would crumble and flake her waxy shell. A research team from Arcadia University just outside Philadelphia hoped that hair follicles or bits of her nails could offer much-needed clues about why she died. But the first test on her fingernails was unsuccessful.

"We were looking for possible cause of death in the form of heavy metals," said Kimberlee Moran, a forensic archaeologist. "X-rays revealed that the Soap Lady had no teeth and that her teeth fell out a long time ago, leaving enough time for the jaw to heal the gaping holes. So we looked into what sorts of toxins could cause one to loose one's teeth. The answer—mercury.

"Hair analysis could not only reveal whether she was exposed to mercury but also if that exposure happened over a period of time. In the end, the nails were tested and the results were negative."

Stay tuned for more on this medical mystery. The opera's not over until the Soap Lady "sings."

FACTLET

SOAP MUMMIES POP up on occasion. Several appeared in Paris two hundred forty years ago when a graveyard, hundreds of years old, was closed. Its dead were exhumed and moved to large underground chambers. Most were bones, but a few had saponified—turned into soap. The doctors on hand came up with a word to describe the waxy material. Thus was born the word *adipocere*—*adipo* (fat) and *cere* (wax). Corpse wax, grave wax, corpse cheese—all describe the outer layer of a soap mummy.

Saponification happens, but only in specific settings. Corpse wax tends to develop in bodies with a high fat content, such as overweight people, women, and children. The burial environment must be both alkaline (the opposite of acidic) and anaerobic (no oxygen.) Moisture helps, but just the liquid in a dead body is enough to get the process going.

FACTLET

BACK WHEN THE SOAP LADY took her baths, soap had two main ingredients: lye and fat. Lye, an alkaline product, was made from ashes and water. Fat came from animals, usually livestock. For generations, until manufacturers took over the job, the woman of the house cooked lye and tallow (animal fat) in kettles to make soap.

When the author of this book was a kid in the 1950s, she asked her grandma to make soap the old-fashioned, pioneer way. Grandma did, and Mom used it in the laundry. She stopped after Dad complained about itchy underwear.

CHAPTER SEVEN

MATERIAL GIRL IN THE AFTERLIFE: CHINA'S LADY DAI

IN 1971, ON ORDERS FROM THEIR COMMUNIST LEADERS, Chinese workers began building an air-raid shelter in Changsha, the capital city of Hunan Province. The shelter was sited at the base of two burial mounds that rose from the ground. No one in memory had messed with the ancient site, called Mawangdui [MAH-WONG-DWAY].

The workers dug a tunnel nearly one hundred feet until they came to some loose soil. When they took a cigarette break, their matches exploded in blue flames. It was "ghost fire," swamp gas from rotting organic matter. Something dead lurked underground.

Archaeologists from nearby Hunan Museum were called in. One felt sure that the workers had found an old vault, a "fire-pit tomb." What was to be an air-raid shelter morphed into an archeological excavation.

The dig began on January 16, 1972, in midwinter, and it moved slowly. After a bulldozer exposed the tomb's entrance, workers used hand tools to clear the site. Labor was in short supply, so high school students helped dig and carry out the dirt in bamboo baskets. Some were so thrilled to be involved, they dug at the soil with their bare hands.

As winter gave way to spring, the kids dug and hauled heavy mud in the rain. But as they dug deeper, the sodden soil gave way to a sticky white clay. They kept at it until yet another layer appeared, this time five-and-a-half tons (five thousand kilos) of charcoal!

First clay, then charcoal—here were all the signs of an ancient burial.

Indeed, underneath the charcoal was a tomb. On top lay bamboo mats, each marked *jia* on the corner, like on bedding at camp. *Jia* [JYAH] is Chinese for "house" or "family." The huge burial chamber below was in fact a house—for the dead. Constructed of sturdy cypress wood, its footprint was the size of a room, sixteen by twenty-two feet (4.9 by 6.7 meters). The burial chamber was about six feet (two meters) tall.

Inside, four oblong compartments bordered a central rectangular box. A translation from a Chinese book about the discovery described the archaeologists' delight: "This is a huge underground treasure house. In the center lies the tremendous coffin, while the surround wing rooms were filled with sparkling treasures. Beneath the mud, every object looked brand-new."

The outside boxes were filled with every kind of object a well-off person would need to enjoy a charming afterlife. The northern box symbolized a sitting room equipped with bamboo mats and silk curtains. There was a short lacquer table, set with tiny dishes. Twenty-three tiny figures crafted of wood stood by, ready to serve as maids, musicians, singers, and dancers.

The west, east, and south boxes stored all that the tomb's occupant would need in the next world. Clothes of silk and baskets and jars filled with seeds and fruit, some for dining, some for curing aches and pains. Boxes of dried beef, venison, and duck. Pottery vessels and bamboo baskets. More than three hundred bamboo strips, to be strung together in a kind of foldup book, inventoried everything packed for the trip.

Some scholars say the tomb builders believed that the soul has two parts: the *Hun* and *Po.* After burial, the *Hun* leaves the grave to rise through heaven into immortality. The *Po*, however, must stay with the body in the tomb. Otherwise, it could descend to the underworld, and no one dared think what horrors could happen then.

What better way to lure a spirit than to offer jars of food, lacquered dishes, drinking cups, silks, and linen? Plus an assortment of *mingqi* [MING-CHEE], translated as "glorious vessels," clay or wood miniatures of pets, barnyard animals, servants, musicians, and cooks—all to provide a comfortable afterlife. *Mingqi* also appeared as inanimate objects like cook stoves, wells, granaries for storing grains, and miniature buildings.

BOXES, BODY, BREAKTHROUGH

The central box held a body encased in four coffins, all coated in shiny lacquer. The archaeologists admired each as they removed it. The innermost box was draped with a banner nearly seven feet (two meters) long, and the box itself was painted with black lacquer and lavished with fine silk and embroidery. They lifted the lid. It was a material world in that coffin.

Hou Liang, the team director, wrote later: "There were two layers of quilts covering her body. They were very beautiful with bright colors and looked brand-new . . . We were all very surprised. Mr. Wang Yuyu . . . who specialized in ancient silk, had never seen such good silk preserved for over two thousand years.

"He was overwhelmed with joy. However, when he reached for the silk, something went wrong. The silk could not be removed. It was as soft as tofu. It looked in sound shape but actually had rotted away."

Under these they found their prize, a silk-wrapped package, tied up with nine silken ribbons. Another archaeologist, Bai Rongjin, looked back: "It was already after midnight. I came at ten o'clock and worked till the latter half of the night to about three o'clock. We cut and cut until we arrived at the top of a piece of hemp cloth. I felt beneath the hemp cloth and found something soft."

It was a body, all right, resting in a weird translucent liquid that turned yellow-brown as the air hit it.

Twenty layers of clothing and materials surrounded the corpse. It took a week for the scientists to work through the wrappings. They worked delicately as a nasty, sour smell wafted from the coffin—and then came a surprise.

What should have been a skeleton was a mummy. Not the taped-up creations of ancient Egypt, but the soft, damp body of a woman, a prime specimen of a natural mummy. For only moments, she was plump with round cheeks and full lips. Then oxygen in the air reacted with her skin, and she began to wither.

A signature seal, an engraved square found in the burial site, identified the dead woman as Xin Zhui [SHIN JWAY], the Marquise of Dai, wife of Li Cang. Indeed, there was a written record of Li Cang. He was the Marquis of Dai who governed Changsha, a county in modern-day Hunan Province. Li Cang died about 186 BCE.

Other burial objects came from the marquis's family. (We pronounce marquis as "mar-KEE." His wife is a marquess [MAR-kwis].)

Clearly, the dead woman had been a grand lady, but exactly who was she?

To find out, more digs followed. The next year, the archaeologists burrowed south and uncovered the tomb with a skeleton of a young man, about thirty, who was buried with things to study: a library of books of silk or bamboo plus maps and paintings. There was a *qin* [CHEEN], a seven-stringed zither plucked with the fingers to make music on a five-note scale. (To Western ears, this sounds like the notes C, D, E, G, and A.)

We assume the man was a soldier, because a sword was entombed with him. Did he work out? An amazing painting

Visitors to China's Hunan Museum honor Lady Dai as they view her remains.

showed forty-four figures of people exercising. "Some were spreading their arms like birds, others are crawling clumsily upward like bears." A popular board game had gone to the grave, as well. Still the tomb offered no clue about the man's name. There was no sign of a signature seal.

Then the team sank a shaft westward of the lady's tomb and uncovered a third burial. This one had been robbed, its occupant gone. Typical of grave robbers, the vandals had left a mess of funerary paraphernalia. But a pair of signature seals, one jade, one bronze, excited everyone. Engraved in the first was a name: Li Cang. The second seal read, "Seal of the Marquis of Dai."

This was good stuff! But the experts looked for more seals to help identify the grave. They raked through baskets of mud looking, until there it was: another bronze seal inscribed "Chancellor of Changsha."

The experts dated the Mawangdui tombs to China's Western Han dynasty, a period of rule from about 206 BCE until 9 CE.

Presumably the young man in the third grave was one of the couple's sons who had died in 168 BCE at about age thirty. The lady Xin Zhui outlived both and died about 158 BCE.

MUMMY POSTMORTEM

The mummy, nicknamed Lady Dai, was a first, the best-preserved human corpse ever discovered. A headline in

China Daily ran: **Chinese Lady Dai Leaves Egyptian Mummies for Dead**. In life, she stood about five feet (one-and-a-half meters) tall and weighed one hundred fifty pounds (sixty-eight kilos). In death, she had kept her hair, half her teeth, and her skin. The blood in her veins was—remarkably—red. There was food in her stomach and intestines. Her fingers and toes still bore their distinctive prints.

The archaeologists loaded the mummy with antiseptic to prevent her decomposing. (To this day, she receives regular shots of a so-called "secret formula" to keep her soft and supple.) The hype kept building until doctors performed an autopsy as an audience of curious scientists and watchful government officials looked on.

Lady Dai was studied inside and out. For a rich girl, the lady had all kinds of ailments. She had heart trouble, a bad gallbladder, and signs of tuberculosis in her lungs. A trio of parasites lurked inside: pinworms and whipworms in her gut and blood flukes (flatworms) in her veins. She had a badly fixed broken arm, lower back problems, and osteoporosis, thinning of the bones. Nevertheless, she lived to the ripe old age of fifty or more. Until the day she ate a melon, Lady Dai was one tough cookie.

She died in summertime. Her autopsy yielded precisely one hundred thirty-eight-and-a-half melon seeds strung out through her digestive system. Melons, of course, ripen when it's hot. Some experts think the melon did the lady in. Her gallbladder, the size of a small pear, was filled with gallstones. Eating the melon might have caused a gallbladder attack. Crushing pain shocked her system, and myocardial infarction followed.

In other words, Lady Dai died from a heart attack.

As telling as it was, the autopsy could not answer a basic question: What had kept the mummy from decomposing in the first place? Obviously, the charcoal and clay surrounding the tomb helped to seal it, as did the protective varnish on the four coffins that helped make them airtight.

Was it that gross-smelling yellow-brown stuff in the bottom of the coffin? Researchers are at odds about this. Some think that groundwater seeped inside the box. Others believe that the lady herself exuded the liquid as she lay in her grave. Still others say that her morticians added a mystery preservative as they prepared her body for burial.

The luxury clothing layered around Lady Dai helped protect her from decomposing, as did the piles of silk garments and blankets stuffed in her innermost coffin. Ironically, they preserved her because they rotted.

As soon as she died, two kinds of bacteria moved in, breaking down Lady Dai's remains, outside and in. Aerobic bacteria on her skin, which depended on oxygen to grow, sucked up oxygen in the coffin. At the same time, the rotting silk oxidized, transforming it into a different substance. This process used up oxygen, too.

No Oxygen = Dead Aerobic Bacteria

The anaerobic bacteria in the lady's intestines, which didn't need oxygen to survive, could have kept eating at her insides. But Lady Dai's very own body fat and proteins created an acidic environment, as did all that rotting silk inside her coffin.

Acid = Dead Anaerobic Bacteria

Therefore, an amazing bit of biochemistry took place inside Lady Dai's tomb:

Dead Aerobic/Anaerobic Bacteria = No More Decomposition

No More Decomposition = A Practically Perfect Lady Dai

A BANNER DAY

Before Lady Dai was sealed away, her mourners lovingly lay a brilliant brown banner, a *feiyi* [fay-EE], atop her innermost coffin. Some think that this striking six-foot-nine-inch masterpiece, tall as a professional basketball player, was carried in her funeral procession. *Feiyi* means "flying garment," and it must have fluttered in the breeze.

When it was discovered, the silk banner was still a rich brown, painted with detailed images of fanciful beasts, sun and moon and clouds, and earthly creatures both human and animal. What was more, it was stuck to the top of the coffin. The experts hand-polished their own slim bamboo tools to peel the banner away from the lid. They worked in dimness, fearing that stronger light could damage the silk. It took hours. In the end, their workmanship rewarded them with a banner that was "priceless—worth several cities."

Archaeologists and art historians pounced on the banner, studying it from top to bottom. They hunted for clues about how people in Lady Dai's day thought about death—and life.

Mostly they agreed that the T-shaped banner portrayed the lady and her hopes for an eternal life in the heavens.

The experts mentally divide the vivid images painted on the banner into three scenes. The bottom scene represents the underworld, where a half-dressed man, standing on a fish, bears the weight of our physical world.

One expert wrote that the banner's midsection shows Lady Dai at home on earth, surrounded by a trio of three female servants behind her and two male servants bowing before her. A different scholar decided, however, that this scene actually shows the earthly farewell to the lady.

Are the mourners bidding Lady Dai's *hun* soul goodbye as it departs for heaven? Lady Dai's cane was buried in her tomb, and the picture seems to say that her soul is taking her cane along. An owl supports a platform bearing two phoenixes, magical birds that bring good virtues to life.

The topmost section, the crossbar of the T, gave the artists more room to paint their mystical concept of heaven. The toad and rabbit both have ties to the moon and its goddess, Chang'e. The three-legged "golden crow," actually black, is linked to the power of the sun.

Dragons play in the scene, and loyal cranes of faithfulness

Lady Dai's banner

flock around the goddess Xi Wangmu, Queen Mother of the West. More cranes drink from a cup of immortality pulled heavenward by two horses-and-riders. Below them are a pair of cats and a pair of men, animal and human guardians of the heavenly realm.

There's a second way of looking at the banner. For centuries, ancient Chinese taught their kids to look at life based on two interlocking forces, yin and yang. (Maybe you've seen a common symbol of yin/yang. It looks like this: ☯)

YIN	YANG
Feminine	Masculine
Dark	Light
Cold	Heat
Water	Fire
North	South

According to this ancient cosmology—how we view the universe—yin and yang have equal power. Neither one is in charge, though they compete constantly. At the same time, they also cooperate. Yin incorporates a bit of yang, and yang embodies a bit of yin. Yin and yang coexist in this world, and after death, in the next.

We can view Lady Dai's banner through the eyes of yin and yang by looking at the larger dragons, whose bodies flow along the sides. Their twisting shapes, stretching from this life to the underworld, play yin and yang. The dragons' bodies meet at the *bi*, a round ornament with a hole in it. There the bodies cross over and swap sides, taking their energy with them. The red-and-gray dragons create a perfect balancing act for the lady's banner.

Today, Lady Dai rests in the Hunan Provincial Museum in her homeland. Her glorious banner is nearby. Museumgoers honor her and ask her blessing. Special flights from Korea and Japan bring worshippers, as well.

FACTLET

AMONG THE SPECIAL foods in a recipe book packed for Lady Dai was caterpillar fungus. Caterpillar fungus, *Cordyceps sinensis,* was brewed and sipped as tea to encourage a long life. This delicacy is still harvested in Nepal and used as Chinese medicine. The fungus invades ghost moth caterpillars, which burrow into the soil and hibernate in winter. Infected caterpillars die and do not transform into moths.

When the soil warms in spring, the fungus grows inside the dead caterpillar, making a ghostly fungal copy of itself inside the caterpillar's shell. When the time is right, the fungus sends a tiny shoot aboveground, a perfect locater for sharp-eyed collectors who can dig it out.

Wildly popular as medicine, caterpillar fungus has been overharvested. In the 2010s, it sold for about fifty thousand dollars per pound (half kilo).

FACTLET

WHAT'S A GALLBLADDER ATTACK? Your gallbladder is a small, pear-shaped organ tucked between your liver and small intestine. Its job is to store bile, a chemical made in your liver that helps your body digest fat. In adults and kids, the gallbladder can fill up with blobs of rocklike masses called gallstones. These can cause inflammation and gallbladder attacks that can feel as painful as heart attacks. But not all gallbladder disease is caused by gallstones. It's fairly common to just have sludge block the duct.

Ask older members of your family if any of them has had gallbladder surgery!

CHAPTER EIGHT

HIGH AND DRY: THE INCA CHILDREN

IN THE EARLY 1500S, SPAIN MADE PLANS TO EXPAND ITS empire across the New World, or so the Americas seemed to the Old-World Spanish.

Across the Atlantic Ocean in South America, a mighty civilization was making a power play of its own. Its people, the Incas, streamed out of their capital high in the Andes Mountains to wage war both north and south.

The Incas were gifted mountaineers, and they used basic engineering to build their cities and temples. They routinely crossed the Andes across high mountain passes that linked lands to the east and west. They conquered other peoples across western South America. From modern-day

The Inca burial site atop Llullaillaco in the Andes Mountains, two thousand two hundred feet above sea level

Colombia in the north to Chile in the south, the Incas ruled along the continent's rocky backbone.

The Incas, like victors everywhere, demanded tribute from the people they conquered. *Tribute*, whose root word comes from *tribe*, took many forms: taxes, crops, livestock, prized shells and minerals, and human slaves. All flowed into the Incan capital city of Cuzco, which conveniently sat in the empire's heartland. There, the Incan emperor, a godlike being who channeled the power and glory of the sun god Inti, received tribute, as was his right.

The most precious form of tribute was a child. Children were sacrificed to Inti, whom the Incas worshipped as the source of their being.

This ritual had a name, *capacocha* [ka-pa-KO-cha]. Attractive, perfectly formed children, some from powerful Incan families, others from conquered tribes, were brought to Cuzco. After a time of preparation, the children were taken in a priestly procession to the tops of the Andes, the very closest that an Incan could get to Inti. There, the children were either killed outright or left to die.

It was a mark of honor for any Incan family to supply a child for *capacocha*. No mother or father or sibling dared show any tears of grief or flashes of anger as a child was taken from their family. Choosing children as tributes was fair game.

TRUTH IS STRANGER THAN FICTION

People from many religions look to the hills or mountains as sources of godly inspiration. The Incas did, and it was on the tops of the highest peaks where they offered their finest sacrifices. They built shrines on stone platforms at monstrously high points. With their eyes on Inti, they dug out graves to entomb their young sacrifices.

It's possible that the Incas believed that these children weren't truly dead. Perhaps the Incas thought their young offerings were transformed into a higher state of being, little gods and goddesses themselves. "Inca sacrifices often involved the child of a chief," said Juan Schobiner, an archaeologist. "The sacrificed child was thought of as a deity, ensuring a tie between the chief and the Inca emperor, who was considered a descendant of the Sun god. The sacrifice also bestowed an elevated status on the chief's family and descendants."

Despite their gifts in engineering and math, the Incas had no written language. What we have as written history comes from the Spaniards who invaded the Incan Empire in 1532 and defeated it three years on. Father Bernabé Cobo, a Roman Catholic missionary, wrote lengthy books about his travels among the Incas. Father Cobo noted:

> Their religion was so firmly established, universally received, and amazingly strict that they offered and sacrificed even their own children . . . In their own minds they believed without any doubt that the sacrifices were not made in vain.

When others read these terrifying tales of child sacrifice, they thought the Spaniards had made them up. Did the Spanish concoct wild stories to justify crushing the Incas?

The tales were true, as archaeologists and explorers discovered five hundred years later. Solid evidence appeared, in the form of . . .

Mummies. Natural mummies. In that cold, windswept environment high atop the Andes, many of those sacrificed children had frozen in time. In 1954, the first mummy—a boy of about twelve—turned up, discovered by a Chilean mule driver and a cobbler who reburied it until they made a successful sale and it ended up in a museum. The naked, frozen corpse of a seven-year-old boy was found on top of another peak in 1985.

It was ten more years until Dr. Johan Reinhard, an American anthropologist, and his climbing partner, Miguel Zírate, discovered the frozen corpse of a young girl as they climbed Peru's Mount Ampato. Named Juanita, the mummy became the Andes' oldest Jane Doe.

Clearly, she was an Incan sacrifice to Inti, but she was an accidental mummy. The Incas who sacrificed her never planned for her body to mummify. They already had plenty back in Cuzco, where the Incas mummified their emperors and took them on parade during religious festivals.

AN ANTHROPOLOGIST FINDS HIS CALLING

As a boy, Johan Reinhard grew up in Illinois farm country, where he learned and dreamed about the great big world.

My early adventures were of hunting, fishing, and camping along Hickory Creek, which flowed through our town. Like some of my friends, I collected fossils and arrowheads, read the Hardy Boys, and experimented with rockets . . . most of which exploded on the launch pad.

He read books about explorers and "was soon dreaming of visiting faraway lands":

> During summers of 1960, 1961, and 1963
> I worked with Southerners on a railroad line
> gang. Our main job was to dig holes by hand, put
> up telegraph poles, and then climb up them to
> add cross arms. The men were all at least four
> years older than I and came from much different
> backgrounds—to put it mildly. To me they were like
> people from another world . . . As a Northerner
> I had to act and talk like they did in order to
> become accepted. Without knowing it, I had begun
> to behave like an ethnographer . . . constantly
> learning more about how these
> strange men thought.

Reinhard learned another lesson atop a "termite-eaten" phone pole that snapped and left him dangling a few feet above ground. "It crystalized in my mind, like nothing else could at that age, the reality that one day I would be dead, and I should not let my life be wasted on doing things I did not find interesting."

RETURN TO THE ANDES

Archaeology expeditions to mountaintops demand money and man/womanpower. In 1999, Reinhard returned to the

Andes with dollars and human help from the National Geographic Society. The team included experts from America, Argentina, and Peru. Reinhard mounted an expedition to Llullaillaco [yu-yai-YA-ko], a volcano twenty-two thousand feet (nearly seven thousand meters) above sea level. Llullaillaco dwarfed better-known mountaintops:

DENALI (MOUNT MCKINLEY), ALASKA
20,237 feet (6,168 meters) tall
MONT BLANC, SWITZERLAND
15,777 feet (4,809 meters) tall
MOUNT FUJIYAMA, JAPAN
12,388 feet (3,776 meters) tall

It was March, autumn in the Andes. Working in snow and seventy-mile-an-hour winds, the explorers spent days tracing a path of disturbed soil—soil that had been excavated and looked different from nearby ground.

It was tough going, and the experts were amazed at how the Incas had managed to build anything so high up. "*Los Incas fueron* hombres" ("The Incas were *men*"), one toughened expert said.

It was touch and go for a week. Cold and wind made it hard to breathe in the oxygen-thin air. A photographer nearly died. Everyone worked without gloves, feeling their way through the soil until their fingers were raw. Nothing was turning up, and things looked bleak—until a pair of brothers began to excavate a circle of stones. They first

A "caravan" of tiny artifacts, circled by a necklace, hinted that a grave lay underneath.

discovered a llama statue made of precious spondylus shell, followed by tiny gold and shell statues of men dressed in real cloth. Then an "alignment of statues" appeared, three more llamas, one of silver and two of spondylus. In front of them, two more male figurines queued up as if to say, "We are leading a caravan of llamas."

A necklace, also of carved spondylus shell, circled the little caravan. Its cord was fashioned of human hair. Excitement mounted; finding this necklace suggested there was a mummy underneath. When they excavated from a different direction, the brothers found it, the frozen corpse of a small child.

In the meantime, a Peruvian guide-turned-explorer excavated a different spot. He had grown up in these mountains, and he seemed to have a sixth sense about things like mummies. Sure enough, his fingers found the white feathers of a full headdress.

"Mummy!" he cried. Five feet (one-and-a-half meters) below his starting point, there was a mummy bundle.

No sooner had he started to clear soil from around the mummy bundle than another set of artifacts appeared in a third location. "Two statues!" called out another team member. "There are gold and spondylus female statues here!"

Three excavations and, now, three mummies, all entombed so high in the mountains they nearly touched the Sun god Inti.

A TRIO OF TOMBS

The tiny caravan had marked the burial of a little boy, no more than four or five years old. As the soil around him was cleaned away, the team saw that his small body had lain uncovered in its grave. His knees were drawn up under his chin, wrapped with cord that forced him into a fetal position like a baby in the womb.

With him were a pair of sandals and a sling. He wore a red tunic, moccasins, and anklets of white fur. As for the rest? The team would keep him frozen until he could be studied in a laboratory.

The white-feathered headdress adorning the second mummy bundle was but one part of a cache of items intended for the afterlife. It was slow going as the one man who could fit into the digging hole began to pass up multiple treasures—statues, pottery, and food such as maize, peanuts, and jerky. These artifacts hinted that the mummy would be female. Finally, the workman picked up the bundle and lifted it up to two others.

Everyone's expectations were confirmed. This mummy was a girl, a teenager. From what they could see, a man's cloak was draped over her, just as a cloak had been draped over Juanita. Off the mountain, they would take their time to study the mummy.

When the team excavated the spot with the two female statues, they ran into solid rock walls. They were working in a hole in the rock called a niche. The Incas had made good use of a natural burial chamber. A strong smell wafted upward, sign of another mummy.

As the lone worker excavated, he found a headdress of glorious multicolored feathers atop a mummy bundle. But the bundle was burned. The metal parts of statues nearby also showed telltale signs—at some point, this grave had been struck by lightning.

The burial niche was so narrow that a student volunteered to be hung by his ankles to work upside down excavating the grave. When it came time to lift out the mummy, the student wrapped his arms around the bundle, shielding it from the rough walls as he was hauled out of the grave.

The small mummy still smelled of burned flesh. As they gently nudged its head cloth, the team was stunned to see the face of a little girl. She looked up at them with a "pensive expression," as if she'd been thinking hard about something. Thankful that the lightning had only taken out her left ear, shoulder, and part of her chest, Johan Reinhard was astonished. He had "looked into the face of an Inca."

The team named her Lightning Girl, *la Niña del Rayo*. The small boy, buried so simply, was simply called Llullaillaco Boy. The teen girl, whose grave outshined the others with its collection of fine cups and plates, precious metal statues, and brilliant textiles, became *La Doncella*, in English, the

With great care, Johan Reinhard revealed the face of Lightning Girl.

Maiden. (Researchers had also given Juanita the nickname "Maiden," which confuses authors who write books about mummies.)

INSIDE INFORMATION

Packed into plastic, snow, and foam insulation, the three dead children left the mountain. They survived a hair-raising series of missteps on the trip, but at last, each mummy was safely seated in its own climate-controlled capsule. *La Doncella*, Lightning Girl, and Llullaillaco Boy now rest in the Museum of High Mountain Archaeology in Salta, Argentina. Only rarely are they removed from their see-through containers.

Radiologists, biochemists, archaeologists, and anthropologists all took a hand in studying the Llullaillaco children. Early CAT scans of *La Doncella*, made before she was unwrapped, showed her sitting cross-legged, her head slumped forward, and her arms in her lap. Between her teeth was a two-and-three-fourths-inch hunk of coca leaves.

There was food in her intestines but not in her stomach; she hadn't eaten at least two-to-seven hours before she died. Nor had she had a bowel movement. Her full rectum proved that. Remarkably, every one of the plates and vessels set around her had stayed in place.

When the researchers unwrapped the Inca children, they were stunned. "We didn't see them when we did the CAT scans because they were covered, but I also helped with the biopsies, and then I saw the Maiden's face," a radiologist, Dr. Carlos Previgliano, recalled. "I was shocked. I was shocked for days because at that time, two of my children were those ages.

"For medicine, mummies are objects," the doctor said. "For us, because of their state (of preservation), we considered them children."

The researchers marveled at the mummies. They looked well fed. Hair samples showed that they ate rich-people foods such as llama meat and maize, what we call corn. Their organs were practically full-size, their tissues like skin, and muscles frozen in near perfection. The CAT scans turned up another amazing find. The mummies were filled with blood, real frozen blood.

Blood had appeared in mummies before, but the environment easily contaminated it. The blood inside these children had been frozen in time. In the future, when technology improves, researchers will extract a minuscule amount in order to look for antibodies to tell them what diseases the children had.

Obviously, the Incas had dealt with these children differently. Despite those white-fur anklets and a silver bracelet on his arm, Llullaillaco Boy, about age seven, had nits and head lice in his straight dark hair. Only a few artifacts were found with him. Lightning Girl, age six or so, was buried with a larger array of funeral objects. She wore fancier dress and a large silver plate across her forehead, which likely attracted that lightning bolt to her.

La Doncella, however, stole the show as best dressed. Atop her two brown mantles lay a brilliant yellow cloth with bold geometric designs. She wore scores of tiny braids all over her head. Was the cactus-thorn comb buried with her used by her stylist? Hair design must have meant something to the Incas. The heavily braided *Doncella* had had a haircut nine months before she died. Those locks of love were bagged up and placed in her grave with her.

Still, CAT scans could not tell the experts how the children died. Earlier discoveries of Andes mummies had shown that those young victims died violent deaths. Juanita, for example, had been bashed in the side of the head. Another little boy of about seven, discovered on another mountain, had vomit on his chest and fecal matter on his clothing.

Llullaillaco Boy was wrapped in rope; perhaps an impatient Incan priest had strangled him when he misbehaved. One expert pointed to traces of blood in the boy's saliva— signs that his small, stressed-out lungs had filled with fluid. She suggested that the boy had died on the trek up the mountain, was wrapped with cord so his body could be carried, and then buried in his waiting grave.

Lightning Girl and *La Doncella* showed no outward signs of trauma, although *La Doncella* had staining on her lips. The experts suspected the girls had died in an altered state of consciousness. At such a high altitude with the air so thin, it would have been easy for the priests to drug them into deadly slumber.

HAIRY DISCOVERIES

Scientists working with the Inca children used improved methods and equipment to answer old questions. About ten years after the burials were discovered, scientists took a fresh look at the children's CAT scans and realized that all

For unknown reasons, Llullaillaco Boy's body was wrapped in cord.

were younger than they'd thought. The little kids were only four or five, and *La Doncella* was thirteen.

The mummies were each removed from their climate-controlled capsules, one by one, for more forensic study. A forensic anthropologist, Dr. Angelique Corthals, plucked single hairs from all three. As an assistant took notes and cameras rolled, the anthropologist spoke as she examined the mummies. She worked quickly; each mummy could be out of its unique capsule only minutes.

The scientist spoke to Llullaillaco Boy and *La Doncella* as she used a long hollow needle to extract muscle cells from their bodies. Those bits of tissue and hair would speak vol-

La Doncella, the Maiden, older and well-fed, seemed to be the highest-ranking mummy among the three found on Llullaillaco.

umes. Corthals noted the stains on the Maiden's mouth, as well as her runny nose.

"As I was working, I was visually five centimeters [two inches] from the maiden. I was gazing at her own eyes. It was a powerful moment . . . I had this feeling coming in me 'Okay, I know you.'" As Corthals returned the mummy to its capsule, she said goodbye and thanked it.

"*Ciao, ciao Doncella. Gracias por todas.*"

Again, the scientist mumbled her apologies to Lightning Girl as she popped out a single lash from the child's eye. "I'm so sorry, little girl."

Corthals and her team analyzed the hair from each mummy. As each hair grew from the kids' scalps, it had created a chemical timeline. For the younger children, whose hair was shorter, the timeline was about nine months long. *La Doncella*'s much longer hair, plus the bagged hair from that earlier haircut, created a timeline twenty-one months long.

The samples showed what foods the children ate. Exactly one year before she died, the Maiden was served an improved diet rich in meat, the same diet that rich Incas enjoyed.

Hair samples also showed how the three kids were medicated. Twelve months before she died, *La Doncella* started "chewing," not tobacco, but leaves of a plant called *coca*. Coca contains cocaine, a medicinal chemical that can kill pain and help with altitude sickness. The Inca priests, it seems, put *La Doncella* on a mountain high.

The younger two were given steady doses of coca and *chicha*, a beer the Incas brewed from maize, in the months before they were sacrificed. But *La Doncella*'s hair showed she'd ingested much more coca, with peak intake about six months before she died. As she approached her death, she drank more and more chicha, as well.

There still lingered the question about stains on the Maiden's mouth. Was there blood? Had she coughed something up from her lungs? What about her runny nose? The team set to work extracting DNA and proteins from her cell tissue. (We cannot know if Lightning Girl was sick. That bolt of electricity had zapped her cells and altered them.)

When the team performed these analyses on *La Doncella*'s tissues, they learned that the teen was sick with an upper respiratory infection during her last days. The culprit was a bacterium from the genus *Mycobacterium*, the same family of nasty microbes that caused tuberculosis in the mummies buried in the Vác church.

In her last days, *La Doncella* probably felt horrible. Chewing that lump of coca might have offered the girl both energy and pain relief as she climbed Llullaillaco. Frequent swigs of chicha would have helped calm her and encourage her body temperature to drop quickly.

La Doncella was most likely either a sleeping beauty or already dead when the priests placed her in her tomb, her funerary goods arranged around her.

There they left her, high and dry.

As mountaintops melt and glaciers recede, many more sacred sites and sacrificial burials will appear in the Andes. Certainly, they are ripe for research—or for looting. As the Incas certainly trafficked in goods (and in children), so do today's black marketers, who have rich customers looking to add jewelry, textiles, and, yes, even mummies to their collections.

FACTLET

A FEW PEOPLE HAVE chosen to be frozen at death, in a process called cryogenics. Their hope is that when a cure is found for what killed them, they can be "thawed" and treated. "Like most medical technologies, this is a chance to live a little bit longer," said a professor who would pay about thirty thousand dollars for the process. When he dies, his body will be placed into a tank of nitrogen held at –202 degrees Fahrenheit (–130 degrees Celsius.).

FACTLET

THE SPELLINGS of *coca* and *cacao* are similar, but they are very different things. Coca comes from the coca plant. Chocolate comes from the cacao tree's beans.

CHAPTER NINE

THE MEDITATING MONKS: HIDING IN PLAIN SIGHT

IT WAS A BEAUTIFUL STATUE, BRONZE AND BOLD, OF THE Buddha. It was a piece of art and an object of respect for Chinese people who called themselves Buddhists. And it was stolen. Or not.

In the 1990s, a sacred bronze statue of a Buddhist monk, likely bought and sold a few times in China, came into the happy hands of a Dutchman, who added it to his private art collection. The statue stayed hidden from public eyes, until its owner decided it needed some freshening up. He hired a Dutch master who restored antiques to fix the statue's cracks and chips.

At first glance, the statue looked like metal, but the restorer discovered its bronze exterior was actually paper maché covered in lacquer and paint. When he pulled away the base of the statue, he saw human skin and human bone. Inside that bronzed monk was a mummified monk.

Holy smoke. A holy man wrapped in a paper shell. What a collector's item!

The "bronze" Buddha statue from China held a big surprise when a CAT scan revealed the mummy of a real monk!

The secret treasure stayed secret until it went on a tour in 2014. A museum curator in Buddhist art and culture and his team used forensic techniques to study the mummy in the same way police study murder victims. Hospital radiologists did CAT scans of the mummy, and a pathologist extracted tissue from its chest and abdomen.

German archaeologist Wilfried Rosendahl said, "During the last weeks he would have started eating less food and drinking only water. Eventually he would have gone into a trance, stopped breathing and died . . . The other monks would have put him close to a fire to dry him out and put him on display in the monastery, we think somewhere in China or Tibet. He was probably sitting for 200 years in the monastery and the monks then realised that he needed a bit of support and preservation, so they put him inside the statue."

The mummy's organs had been removed, and it was stuffed with paper. Chinese text linked the mummy to a Buddhist master documented in history. For a time, scholars believed that the bronzed mummy was the body of the Buddhist master Liuquan, a Chinese holy man who lived about one thousand years ago.

But when his striking image hit Chinese newspapers, villagers claimed that the statue had been stolen from their local temple back in 1995. They said that the mummy was one

Zhanggong Zushi [JAHNG-GUHNG JOO-SHEE], a beloved monk who lived about the same time as Liuquan.

The statue's Dutch owner yanked the mummy off the museum circuit and took it home. News reports said that he was willing to return the monk to its temple, but only if the Chinese could prove his identity.

No matter who he was, the mummy in bronze raised questions:

- Was this Buddhist monk a special guy?
- Was he one of the enlightened ones, a monk who had reached the highest state of being?
- Did he hope to mummify?

BUDDHISM—A SIMPLE INTRODUCTION

It will help you to know a bit about Buddhism. Buddhism is not so much a religion as it is a way of living. It had its start in India about five hundred years before Jesus Christ, when a prince of huge wealth, Siddhartha Gautama, left his cushy home to live as a monk. The princely monk embarked on a life journey in order to make peace with his soul.

This monk never stopped thinking or asking deep questions about what it meant to be a human being in an ever-changing universe. He often stopped to meditate, to clear his mind and sit quietly, like a lotus flower, with his legs crossed and arms relaxed.

Siddhartha Gautama spent many years in struggle, in body and in spirit, as he asked life's big questions. Over that time, he came to believe that suffering lies at the heart of the human condition and can never be escaped. We are born, we suffer, and we die. Our souls appear again in another body—human or animal—in an endless journey of reincarnation.

But then on a day that started out like any other, Siddhartha Gautama sat under a tree to meditate. As he sat there quietly, his entire being flashed with insight, what we call an epiphany. The holy man realized that people *can* rise above suffering, but how?

The only way to live life is to live without fear.

This new thinking blew his mind. Now Siddhartha Gautama understood how to live his days: to live without fear, to prepare his soul for the final step of its journey, to enter nirvana. There, his soul would enjoy the perfect inner peace of enlightenment. (Do not confuse nirvana with the popular notion of heaven as a place where streets are paved with gold and angels play harps. Nirvana is explained more as a state of calm, where no flames of greed, anger, or hate can burn. There is no more "I." There is only nirvana, being at one with the universe.)

When Siddhartha Gautama died, he was remembered as a Buddha, an enlightened one. Buddhists teach that there have been other Buddhas and that more will come. But Siddhartha Gautama is known through history as *The* Buddha. Buddhists—and there are many kinds—follow the Buddha's Eightfold Path to right living.

Buddhists teach that life and death are part of an eternal, universal cycle of change. Everything has a cause, and everything has an effect. People live and die, mountains crumble, and galaxies fade away. Siddhartha Gautama taught that every person—even the worst jerk you can think of—has a spark of the Buddha. That spark offers every single person a chance to reach enlightenment and means that we must treat others as we would treat ourselves.

THE MUMMIES WHO AREN'T

About the same time the bronzed monk lived in China, Buddhist monks in Japan followed their own bizarre paths to glory. They got so good at meditation and going hungry that they mummified themselves.

They called themselves *sokushinbutsu* [so-ku-shee-en-boo-TSU]. These atypical monks practiced extreme self-denial. Some (but not all) Buddhists might say they reached nirvana by trapping their souls inside their bodies to become "Living Buddhas." Archaeologists would say that these monks starved themselves to death.

THE SOKUSHINBUTSU PATH TO LIVING BUDDHAHOOD

1. Be a man. Women not allowed.
2. Remove all grains and beans from diet. Eat only nuts, seeds, pine bark, and evergreen tree roots in order to shrink body fat and muscle to practically nothing. Meditate.
3. Gradually stop drinking water. Sip tea brewed from the sap of the urushi tree. Vomit and sweat and dry out. Meditate.
4.. Move to a sacred mountain for one thousand days. Take cold water baths three times daily. Walk a trail to a sacred shrine every day, rain or shine, sick or dying. Meditate.
5. At the end of three years' time, enter a double coffin in a small stone chamber. Bring a breathing tube and a bell. Assume the lotus position. Meditate. Others will cover the chamber.
6. Ring the bell once each day. Meditate.

One day, that bell wouldn't ring. The brother monks would take this as a hopeful sign that their friend was reaching nirvana. But they wouldn't know for sure until they opened the

Daijuku Bosatsu Shinnyokai Shonin, a Japanese monk who died at ninety-six, is venerated as *sokushinbutsu*, a Living Buddha, in a Buddhist temple.

stone chamber months later. If they found a mummy, the candidate had become *sokushinbutsu*.

Mummified monks are rare. In Japan, twenty-one examples have survived, as it were, over the last one thousand years. They are housed in Buddhist temples mostly in Japan's north. There, the faithful have come to these shrines to pray for help and ask for favors, as cycles of bad harvests, widespread hunger, and the crush of harsh rulers and high taxes weighed them down.

Temple abbots will tell you that the monks are Living Buddhas. *Sokushinbutsu* are regularly cleaned and redressed in fresh white undergarments and bright saffron robes.

Their very presence is a lesson to others. "It is the principle of 'I suffer so that you might live,'" said Yugaku Endo, a chief priest of the Dainichibo Temple in Japan.

FACTLET

ABOUT THAT URUSHI TREE sap that Japan's mummy monks brewed into tea and drank to dry themselves out? The urushi tree is also China's so-called lacquer tree. Its botanical name is *Toxicodendron vernicifluum*, and toxic it is.

Remember the glossy lacquer coating on Lady Dai's coffins? That was distilled from lacquer tree sap. Its active ingredient is urushiol, an oil that makes us itch. Urushiol makes its North American appearance in—what else—poison ivy!

FACTLET

IN 2012, A NINETY-FOUR-YEAR-OLD Buddhist monk died and was mummified in southeast China. His corpse was washed, treated, and placed in a large jar. Three years later, everyone was pleased to see that the monk, Fu Hou, had mummified. He was bathed in alcohol, wrapped in gauze, lacquered, and covered in layers of pricey gold leaf. Dressed and encased, Fu Hou awaits visitors who visit his mountain temple.

CHAPTER TEN

WRAP-UP: THE GOOD, THE NOT AS GOOD, AND THE INFAMOUS

SCORES OF MUMMIES HAVE MADE HEADLINES OVER THE years. The honored—and dishonorable—dead draw fans for all kinds of reasons. There are popes and politicians, divas and dictators, and saints and sinners. Mummified people have been found dead at home, too.

THE REVOLUTIONARY MUMMY OF VLADIMIR LENIN

Depending on your view of world history, Russia's Vladimir Lenin was either a hero or a villain. In 1917, Lenin became the grand master of the Bolshevik Revolution that overthrew Russia's newborn democracy. He rose to lead a different nation, the Union of Soviet Socialist Republics. He

ordered the murder of the Romanovs, Russia's royal family, and anyone else who stood against the revolution. But to his fellow Communists, and to Russia's hungry peasants and workers, Lenin seemed like Superman, the hero of the Russian Revolution.

Lenin died at age fifty-three in 1924 in the cold of winter. His body didn't begin to decay for several months, which gave the government time to decide what to do with it. The new Soviet society, though officially denying God's existence, embalmed Vladimir Lenin and enshrined him inside their stronghold, the Kremlin.

Today, a team of Russian scientists called the Mausoleum Group treats his body to regular chemical baths in a kind of ongoing scientific experiment.

THE ELEGANT EMBALMING OF EVA PERÓN

When the young first lady of Argentina, Eva Perón, died of cancer in 1952, long lines of mourners crowded the streets of Buenos Aires to view her specially prepared body. She was only thirty-three years old. In death she looked nearly as lovely as when she'd lived.

Gossip said that Eva's husband, President Juan Perón, had Lenin's grand corpse in mind when he ordered Evita's body to be preserved for all time.

When Juan Perón lay in state in a closed casket (*below*) in 1974, Eva Perón's mummy was laid there, as well.

The embalmer assured Perón that he could touch her face. "Don't be afraid," he said. "She's as whole, *intacta*, as when she was alive." The embalmer did a very good job. Eva's mummy became a symbol of power for the Peronists.

When Perón's enemies toppled him from power, they hid Eva's mummy. For the next sixteen years, her body endured a series of secret journeys, eventually ending up in a secret Italian grave.

Juan Perón reclaimed Eva's corpse in 1971. Perón and his new wife, Isabel, kept Eva's mummy on a dining room table. Every day, Isabel combed its fair hair. Newspapers later reported that Isabel would lie down beside the mummy, hoping that she would channel Eva's mysterious enchantment.

THE HEAVENLY HOST OF INCORRUPTIBLES

For two thousand years, Roman Catholics and Eastern Orthodox Christians have venerated the saints, their holiest women and men. The bodies of the sainted dead were treated with special care and respect. Over that time, they began to believe that a saint's body could have miraculous powers. Relics (body parts) of dead saints lie under the altar of practically every Catholic and Orthodox church in the world.

Sometimes, when the tombs of these sacred dead were opened, the bodies hadn't turned to bones. The church fathers called them incorruptibles.

In the 1200s, a humble servant named Zita, who filled her life with good works, was buried under the church floor in her town of Lucca, Italy. Legends about Zita's goodness put her on the path to sainthood.

Imagine the shock and awe when Zita's coffin was opened in 1580. Her body hadn't decomposed. St. Zita was elevated to rare standing as one of the Church's incorruptibles. In other words, she'd become a natural mummy, but in 1580, no one had figured that out.

Today, St. Zita lies in her glass casket in Lucca's Basilica of San Frediano.

The same happened with a more modern saint, Catherine Labouré, a French nun who died in 1876. When she began the road to sainthood, the Catholic Church exhumed her body in 1933. Like Zita, Catherine had mummified. Her

body lies in the Chapel of Our Lady of the Miraculous Medal, Paris.

There are many examples of incorruptibles among the saints: St. Vincent de Paul, St. Bernadette Soubirous, St. John Bosco, and St. Catherine of Genoa. In the late 1900s, the Vatican invited an Italian pathologist, Ezio Fulcheri, to assist in preserving the corpse of a cardinal, a beloved churchman among the faithful in Ukraine.

Fascinated with the history and tradition behind incorruptibles, the pathologist began to study them. Dr. Fulcheri discovered the truth. At some point, human hands had worked to preserve many of them. Others, such as Zita, had mummified naturally.

But in the eyes of this man of science, these sacred dead still deserved their sainthood.

FACTLET

EVEN NOW, SOME PEOPLE sign up to be mummified after they die. A religious group in Salt Lake City, Utah, carries out their last wishes inside a metal pyramid, home to Summum. There, Summum followers meet, meditate, and mummify.

Summum is a mix of religion, mysticism, and science fiction. *Summum* is Latin for "the sum total of all creation." Followers believe that mummification eases the way for a person's soul to move into the afterlife. They also claim that their mummies retain cell tissue, perfect for cloning when the time is right. At a price of sixty-seven thousand dollars, about the cost of two years at a private college, mummification doesn't come cheap. It's much cheaper to mummify one's pet for four thousand dollars.

FACTLET

RUSSIA'S MAUSOLEUM GROUP takes care of other dead leaders. Again, depending on who writes the history textbook, all were either great men or evil villains. There's Ho Chi Minh of North Vietnam (died 1969), the People's Republic of China's Mao Zedong (died 1976), and father-son dictators of North Korea Kim Il Sung (died 1994) and Kim Jong Il (died 2011).

A mausoleum (mah-sah-LEE-um) is a tomb, usually built above ground, to house the dead. All these specially preserved bodies are entombed in mausoleums.

Tut's mask allows us to look in the eyes of a boy king.

AFTERWORD

WHEN I WAS A KID GROWING UP IN OAK PARK, ILLINOIS, my family often visited the Field Museum of Natural History in downtown Chicago. To this day, two exhibits stay with me—dinosaur skeletons and mummies. As a young adult in 1977, I was one among thousands who lined up to view the *Treasures of Tutankhamun* at the Smithsonian Museum in Washington, DC.

When I saw them, I appreciated that both dinosaurs and mummies had once been living, breathing creatures (not at the same time, of course ☺). But as I stood in the halls of those magnificent museums, their lives and times felt very far and distant from my own. I was there to look at them, read about them, and learn from them. That's why I still visit museums.

Today, there are passionate debates between archaeologists and those they "archaeologize." Native American groups and others object to displaying bodies of dead people for others to view.

When the Canadian Museum of Civilization (now the Canadian Museum of History) displayed the remains of Yde Girl, her appearance on a T-shirt disgusted many. A newspaper reporter presumed that "there would be no tasteless souvenirs sold in the museum gift shop. T-shirts displaying images of rotting corpses apparently passed the taste test and are on sale." ("Rotting corpses" isn't quite accurate, as a researcher noted, but you get the idea.)

Professor Margaret Bruchac, an Indigenous archaeologist from the University of Pennsylvania, explained to me that every culture has its own beliefs and ways of dealing with the dead. She wrote:

> Even ancient hominids (including Neanderthals) practiced burial rituals. Most Indigenous people today (Native American, First Nations, Aboriginal Australians, and others) believe that human burial sites should never be disturbed. They also believe that disturbing the dead can bring harm to the living. Many religious groups (Catholic, Jewish, Muslim, etc.) similarly consider ancestral burial sites to be sacred ground.

Since the 1990s, an increasing number of museums and research labs have honored the wishes of Native people in North and South America, Australia, and New Zealand. The remains of thousands of aboriginal people have been returned to their ancestral homelands for burial.

Rima Eriknova, the museum director who cares for the Altai Princess in Siberia, felt torn about putting her on display. The director preferred that the mummy be reburied:

> Many Altay people couldn't look at her. It's not our custom to mix with the dead. Once you have been buried no one should disturb you. Yet, as Director of the museum, I am obliged to keep her here, to display her. But nonetheless, I believe she should be reburied, returned to where she came from.

Scientists argue that there is much more to learn about aboriginal people, and that their work must continue. They also point out that Native American burial sites attract grave robbers. Why not, they say, continue to shield these sites from vandals by doing fieldwork there and protecting what they find?

Dr. Natalia Polosmak, the archaeologist who discovered the Altai Princess, mourned the ban in Altay that prevented her from returning to do more archaeology. "Since our arrival, the Ukok [princess] returned to life and started revealing its secrets. We have begun to tell its story. So we were really upset when they introduced this ban. It meant curtailing this historic step forward. That is a shame."

The quarrels between outside researchers and peoples of Native ancestry go on. In an email to me, Professor Bruchac suggested a way to move forward:

> It is always difficult to balance scientific desires and cultural desires when it comes to the practice of archaeology. Scientists who practice 'Indigenous archaeology' suggest that the best approach is to always consult with, work closely with, and respect the needs of the descent community before conducting any kind of study of ancestral dead.

The archaeologists I encountered as I wrote this book hold deep respect for those they study. Professor Polosmak said this:

> The fact that I dug her up ... gives me an uneasy responsibility ... Although we know the soul is immortal and the body is only a shell ... something the Pazyryk believed ... it always provokes a feeling ... of unease, pity, and sadness when you see a once great woman ... about whom you know so much ... lying there in front of you.

Respect—something for *us all* to remember. Respect for the dead, and for the living, too.

GLOSSARY

CAT SCAN—X-ray pictures that reveal cross sections of the body, as though you are looking at slices of a loaf of bread.

CELL—Cells are the building blocks of life. Trillions of cells in humans provide the body's structure, convert nutrients into energy, and perform special functions. Cells also contain chromosomes, the body's hereditary information.

CHROMOSOME—Chromosomes, threadlike structures, are inside the cells of all living things. Composed of protein and DNA, chromosomes carry genes, hereditary information passed from parents to offspring.

DNA—DNA molecules carry the genetic codes of all living things, from single-celled creatures to human beings. The genetic code controls how a living thing will look, act, and reproduce. Scientists explain that DNA molecules are arranged in a double helix, which look like a twisting ladder. DNA's chemical name is deoxyribonucleic acid.

FORENSICS—Use of scientific methods in solving crimes.

GENE—A basic unit of heredity that a parent passes to a child. Genes are short pieces of DNA that determine your features such as eye color, hair color, height, and sex. Genes organize themselves onto chromosomes.

GENETICS—The science of heredity, how all living things pass on their traits to their offspring.

GENOME—The full set of genetic material in an organism.

HEREDITY—The passing of traits to offspring. This is the process by which an offspring cell or organism acquires the characteristics of its parent cell or organism.

MRI—*Magnetic resonance imaging* allows doctors and scientists noninvasive views of tissues in the body, that is, without doing surgery. Unlike X-ray and CAT scans, MRIs do not require radiation.

RADIOCARBON DATING—In dead plants and animals, radiocarbon decays at a steady rate. Half of it is gone about five thousand seven hundred thirty years after death. By measuring the amount of radiocarbon remaining in the bone or tissues of a dead person, an archaeologist can establish when that person died.

RADIOLOGIST—A doctor who has special training in reading X-rays, CAT scans, and MRIs in order to diagnose illness or injury.

NOTES

INTRODUCTION

vi "...was bared of his wrappings and brought once more to the light of day ..." Kathleen L. Sheppard, "Between Spectacle and Science: Margaret Murray and the Tomb of the Two Brothers," *Science in Context* 25, no. 4 (2012): 525, doi.org/10.1017/S0269889712000221.

vi "Before that,..." Kathleen Sheppard, "Between Specatacle and Science," 525.

CHAPTER ONE: WHAT'S BEHIND CURTAIN NUMBER ONE?

3 "thunderstruck" Evan Hadingham, "The Mummies of Xinjiang," *Discover* (April 1994), discovermagazine.com/1994/apr/themummiesofxinj359.

3 "He looked like my brother Dave sleeping there ..." Heather Pringle, "The Curse of the Red-Headed Mummy," excerpt from *The Mummy Congress* (New York: Hyperion, 2001): 32.

9 "That very afternoon, I became an archaeologist." Heather A. Davis, "Q&A with Victor Mair," *Penn Current*, February 3, 2011, penncurrent .upenn.edu/node/2900.

13 "The people of the past ..." Davis, "Q&A."

16 "He's the most resplendently garbed mummy I've ever seen ..." Samuel Hughes, "When West Went East," *Pennsylvania Gazette* (January/ February 2011): 47.

CHAPTER TWO: THE MOCHE MOMMY AND MANY MORE MUMMIES

21 "Dumbfounded ..." John Verano in conversation with the author, May 3, 2017.

27–28 "Artificial mummification provided a resting place ..." Tom D. Dillehay, "Selective complexity and adaptive mortuary behavior," proceedings of the National Academy of Sciences, pnas.org/ content/109/37/14722.full.pdf.

29 "Once you die, you naturally mummify ..." "Why the South American Chinchorro People Made the First Mummies," *PRI's The World*, August 13, 2012, pri.org/stories/2012-08-13/why-south-american-chinchorro -people-made-first-mummies.

32 "When the sacrifice ... We had identified him in 1972, ..." Walter Alva

and Christopher B. Donnan, "Tales from a Peruvian Crypt," *Natural History* 103, no. 5 (May 1994): 26–35.

CHAPTER THREE: ÖTZI THE ITALIAN ICEMAN

35 "*Schau mal, was da liegt*" David Klaubert, "Wir dachten, das sei ein toter Bergsteiger," *Frankfurter Allgemeine*, September 19, 2011, faz.net/aktuell /gesellschaft/umwelt/oetzi-finderin-erika-simon-wir-dachten-das-sei -ein-toter-bergsteiger-11290181.html.

39 "And if the dating is revised . . ." Konrad Spindler, *The Man in the Ice: The Discovery of a 5,000-Year-Old Body Reveals the Secrets of the Stone Age*, translated by Ewald Osers (New York: Harmony Books, 1995): 7.

40 "Scientists Enthralled by Bronze Age Body" Brenda Fowler, "Scientists Enthralled by Bronze Age Body," *New York Times*, October 1, 1991, C1.

40 "Should Just Anybody Be Allowed to Stare?" Brenda Fowler, "Should Just Anybody Be Allowed to Stare?" *New York Times*, June 16, 1996, E6.

40 "Lessons in Iceman's Prehistoric Medicine Kit" John Noble Wilford, "Lessons in Iceman's Prehistoric Medicine Kit," *New York Times*, December 8, 1998, nytimes.com/1998/12/08/science/lessons-in-iceman -s-prehistoric-medicine-kit.html.

43 "He died quite peacefully" Vera Haller, "Modern Marketing Embraces Iceman; Bronze Age Mummy Found on Glacier Moved to Italian Museum Amid Hoopla," *Washington Post*, April 12, 1998, A19.

46 "Historic records highlight the fatal destiny . . ." Patrizi Pernter, Paul Gostner, Eduard Egarter Vigl, and Frank Jakobus Rühli, "Radiologic proof for the Iceman's cause of death (ca. 5'300 BP)," *Journal of Archaeological Science* 34, no. 11 (November 2007): 1784–1786.

46 "big, hollow organ" David Murdock and Brando Quilici, "Iceman Murder Mystery," PBS's *NOVA*/National Geographic Television, October 26, 2011, pbs.org/wgbh/nova/ancient/iceman-murder-mystery.html.

52 "pathologies and damages" Maya Wei-Haas, "An Artist Creates a Detailed Replica of Ötzi, the 5,300-Year-Old 'Iceman,'" Smithsonian .com, February 17, 2016, smithsonianmag.com/science-nature/artist -creates-detailed-replica-otzi-5300-year-old-iceman-180958151.

CHAPTER FOUR: BOGGY BODIES IN TANNING BEDS

58 "a flap of dark, tanned skin . . ." Chris Long, "Lindow Man: Gruesome Discovery who Became 'International Celebrity,'" *BBC News*, August 3, 2014, bbc.com/news/uk-england-28589151.

60 "This is going to sound daft . . ." Jason Donaghy, text message to Christine Bissmeyer and relayed to the author, November 21, 2016.

61 "The bog mummies are only preserved . . ." Nielsen, Ole. Email to the author, January 4, 2018.

62 "But not all of these injuries . . ." Julia Farley, comment to the author, December 11, 2017.

62 "We don't know . . ." Julia Farley, comment to the author, December 11, 2017.

63 "Here we noted more . . ." Anne Ross and Don Robins, "Face to Face with a Druid," *New Scientist* 116, no. 1591 (December 17, 1987): 19.

66 "We found things like blackboard rubbers . . ." Lynn Dicks, "Mystery in the Mire," *New Scientist* 117, no. 2382 (February 15, 2003): 38–41.

68 "for a moment returned from another world, . . ." P. V. Glob, *The Bog People: Iron-Age Man Preserved* (Ithaca: Cornell University Press, 1969): 18.

69 "all water in the tissue . . ." Nielsen, Ole. Email to the author, January 4, 2018.

69–70 "The four-centimeter-long hair . . ." Ibid.

71 "The reason was that her body was found . . ." Vincent van Vilsteren, comment to the author, December 20, 2017.

72 "rather like a dead cat . . ." Vincent van Vilsteren, e-mail message to the author, November 30, 2016.

76 "The killings tend to be excessive . . ." James O'Shea, "Bog bodies Are Kings Sacrificed by Celts, Says Expert," irishcentral.com/news/bog-bodies-are-kings-sacrificed-by-celts-says-expert-129289548-237410131.

77 "The Goddess had a threefold nature," Eamonn Kelly, comment to the author, January 8, 2018.

77 "I see these bodies as ambassadors . . ." Matt McGrath, "World's Oldest Bog Body Hints at Violent Past," *BBC News*, September 24, 2013, bbc.com/news/science-environment-24053119.

78 "inaugurated . . . Boundaries were perceived . . ." Eamonn Kelly, comments to the author, January 8, 2018.

79 "Bog butter is . . ." Eamonn Kelly, comment to the author, January 8, 2018.

CHAPTER FIVE: ARM TATTOO IN INKY BLUE: THE ALTAI PRINCESS

85–86 "Here, when the king dies, they dig a grave, . . ." Junhi Han, *Preservation of the Frozen Tombs of the Altai Mountains*, translated by Lise

Sellem and David Tresilian, Flemish/UNESCO Cultural Trust Fund (March 2008): 69.

88 "In the deep, long winter of Novosibirsk, ..." Natalia Polosmak, "A Mummy Unearthed from the Pastures of Heaven," *National Geographic* 186, no. 4 (1994): 95.

91 "In the crook of the lady's knee ..." Natalia Polosmak, "A Mummy Unearthed," 99.

92 "I couldn't help but wonder ..." Natalia Polosmak. "A Mummy Unearthed from the Pastures of Heaven," National Geographic 186, no. 4 (1994): 102.

96 "The soul is somewhere else ..." "Siberian Princess Reveals Her 2,500 Year Old Tattoos," *Siberian Times*, August 14, 2012, siberiantimes.com /culture/others/features/siberian-princess-reveals-her-2500-year-old -tattoos.

CHAPTER SIX: SICK: MUMMY MEDICAL MYSTERIES

107 "conclusive evidence of TB" Michael Pallen, e-mail to the author, December 19, 2016.

107 "It was a tragic life" Ildiko Pap as quoted in Dana Bartholomew, "'Mummies of the World' Exhibit at California Science Center," *Daily News*, June 25, 2010, dailynews.com/2010/06/25/mummies-of-the -world-exhibit-at-california-science-center.

107-108 "One of the reasons I don't want to be a docter." Janice Habuda, "'Mummies of the World' Puts Human Face to Exhibit at Buffalo Museum of Science," *Buffalo News*, April 13, 2014.

108 "They're not objects ..." Janice Habuda, "Mummies of the World."

109 "I give the bodies ..." Anna N. Dhody, "The Curious Case of Mrs. Ellenbogen," *Expedition* 58, no. 2 (Fall 2016): 47.

109 "Old and probably ugly ..." Anna Dhody, "Curious Case," 47.

111 "We were looking for possible cause of death ..." Kimberlee Moran, comment to the author, December 23, 2017.

CHAPTER SEVEN: MATERIAL GIRL IN THE AFTERLIFE: CHINA'S LADY DAI

114 "... ghost fire ..." Bonn-Muller, Eti. "Entombed in Style: The Lavish Afterlife of a Chinese Noblewoman." Archaeology, May/June 2009, www.globaleditorialservices.com/wp-content/uploads/2010/10/ Entombed_in_Style.pdf.

115 "fire-pit tomb" Zhang Dongxia and Xu Lei, *The Legend of Mawangdui* (Beijing: China Intercontinental Press, 2007): 52.

115–116 "This is a huge underground treasure house ..." Zhang Dongxia, *Legend of Mawangdui*, 55.

117 "There were two layers of quilts covering her body ..." Zhang Dongxia, *Legend of Mawangdui*, 58.

118 "It was already after midnight ..." Zhang Dongxia, *Legend of Mawangdui*, 59.

120 "Some were spreading their arms like birds ..." Zhang Dongxia, *Legend of Mawangdui*, 73.

121 "Chinese Lady Dai Leaves Egyptian Mummies for Dead" Yu Chunhong, "Chinese Lady Dai Leaves Egyptian Mummies for Dead," *China Daily*, updated August 25, 2004, chinadaily.com.cn/english/doc/2004-08/25/content_368631.htm.

121 "secret formula" Eti Bonn-Muller, "Entombed in Style," *Archaeology* 62, no. 3 (May–June 2009): 40–43.

124 "priceless—worth several cities" "T-shaped painting on silk from Xin Zhui's tomb," Hunan Provincial Museum, www.hnmuseum.com/en/content/t-shaped-painting-silk-xin-zhui's-tomb.

CHAPTER EIGHT: HIGH AND DRY: THE INCA CHILDREN

131–132 "Inca sacrifices often involved the child of a chief ..." Liesl Clark, "The Sacrificial Ceremony," PBS's *NOVA*, originally broadcast November 1998, pbs.org/wgbh/nova/ancient/sacrificial-ceremony.html.

132 "Their religion was so firmly established ..." Father Bernabé Cobo, *Inca Religion and Customs,* translated and edited by Roland Hamilton (Austin: University of Texas Press, 1990): 8.

133 "My early adventures were of hunting ..." Johan Reinhard, personal website, johanreinhard.net/Educational-Resources/archives.

134 "During summers of 1960 ..." Johan Reinhard, *Discovering the Inca Ice Maiden* (Washington, DC: National Geographic Children's Books, 1998): 108.

134 "termite-eaten ... It crystalized in my mind ..." Johan Reinhard, *Discovering*, 109.

135 "*Los Incas fueron* hombres" Johan Reinhard, *Discovering*, 299.

136 "alignment of statues" Johan Reinhard, *Discovering*, 297.

137 "Mummy!" Johan Reinhard, *Discovering*, 299.

137 "Two statues! . . . There are gold . . ." Johan Reinhard, *Discovering*, 299.

139 "pensive expression . . . looked into the face . . ." Johan Reinhard, *Discovering*, 308–309.

140–141 "We didn't see them when we did the CAT scans . . ." Melody Brumble, "Researcher Helps Unwrap Mystery of 3 Incan Children," *Shreveport Times*, August 15, 2013, usatoday.com/story/tech/2013/08/15 /volcan-llullaillaco-mummies/2660113.

145 "*Ciao, ciao Doncella.*" Pamela Caragol Wells, *Child Mummy Sacrifice* (Washington, DC: National Geographic Video, 2010), DVD.

145 "I'm so sorry . . ." Ibid.

148 "Like most medical technologies . . ." Bob Woodruff, "Life on Ice: The World of Crazy Cryogenics," abcnews.go.com/Health/life-ice-world -crazy-cryogenics/story?id=14167348.

CHAPTER NINE: THE MEDITATING MONKS: HIDING IN PLAIN SIGHT

151 "During the last weeks . . ." Nick Squires, "Mummified Monk Revealed Inside 1,000-Year-Old Buddha Statue," *Telegraph*, February 24, 2015, telegraph.co.uk/news/worldnews/europe/germany/11432544 /Mummified-monk-revealed-inside-1000-year-old-Buddha-statue .html.

156 "It is the principle of 'I suffer so that you might live'" Cathy Newman, "Pick Your Poison—12 Toxic Tales," *National Geographic*, May 2005.

CHAPTER TEN: WRAP-UP: THE GOOD, THE NOT AS GOOD, AND THE INFAMOUS

161 "Don't be afraid . . ." Nicholas Fraser and Marysa Navarro, *Evita: The Real Life of Eva Perón* (New York: W. W. Norton, 1980): 169–170.

164 "the sum total of all creation." Welcome to Summum, summum.us/about /welcome.shtml.

AFTERWORD

168 "there would be no tasteless souvenirs sold . . ." Heather Gill-Robinson, "Bog Bodies on Display," *Journal of Wetland Archaeology* 4, no. 1 (2004): 111–116, doi.org/10.1179/jwa.2004.4.1.111.

168 "Even ancient hominids (including Neanderthals) practiced burial rituals . . ." Margaret Bruchac, e-mail message to the author, July 21, 2017.

169 "Many Altay people couldn't look at her . . ." "Ice Mummies: Siberian Ice Maiden," *NOVA* Transcripts, November 24, 1998, pbs.org/wgbh/nova /transcripts/2517siberian.html.

169 "Since our arrival, the Ukok returned to life . . ." "Ice Mummies," *NOVA* Transcripts.

170 "It is always difficult to balance scientific desires and cultural desires . . ." Margaret Bruchac, e-mail, July 21, 2017.

170 "The fact that I dug her up . . ." "Indo-European mummy in the Altai— Part 5," BBC Learning, youtube.com/watch?v=df7ZGHMFtNY.

SELECT BIBLIOGRAPHY

Denotes books and websites suitable for young readers

General Books and Websites about Mummies

Deem, James. "Mummy Tombs," mummytombs.com/main.mummy.html.

*———. "The World of James Dean," website of children's author of several books about archeology, jamesmdeem.com.

Pringle, Heather. *The Mummy Congress: Science, Obsession, and the Everlasting Dead.* New York: Hyperion, 2001.

*Sloan, Chris. *Mummies: Dried, Tanned, Sealed, Drained, Frozen, Embalmed, Stuffed, Wrapped, and Smoked . . . And We're Dead Serious.* Washington, DC: National Geographic Children's Books, 2010.

Wieczorek, Alfried, and Wilfried Rosendahl, eds. *Mummies of the World.* New York: Prestel, 2010.

INTRODUCTION

Murray, Margaret Alice. *The Tomb of the Two Brothers.* Manchester: Sherratt & Hughes, 1910.

Sheppard Kathleen L. "Between Spectacle and Science: Margaret Murray and the Tomb of the Two Brothers." *Science in Context 25*(4), 525–549 (2012).

CHAPTER ONE: WHAT'S BEHIND CURTAIN NUMBER ONE?

Barber, Elizabeth Wayland. *The Mummies of Ürümchi.* New York: W. W. Norton, 1999.

Davis, Heather A. "Q&A with Victor Mair," *Penn Current,* February 3, 2011, penncurrent.upenn.edu/node/2900.

Hadingham, Evan. "The Mummies of Xinjiang," *Discover* (April 1994), discovermagazine.com/1994/apr/themummiesofxinj359.

Hughes, Samuel. "When West Went East," *Pennsylvania Gazette* (January/ February 2011), upenn.edu/gazette/0111/feature2_1.html.

Mair, Victor H. "The Mummies of East Central Asia," penn.museum /documents/publications/expedition/PDFs/52-3/mair.pdf.

Mallory, J. P., and Victor H. Mair. *The Tarim Mummies: Ancient China and the Mystery of the Earliest Peoples from the West.* London: Thames & Hudson, 2000.

Pringle, Heather, *The Mummy Congress: Science, Obsession, and the Everlasting Dead*. New York: Hyperion, 2001.

CHAPTER TWO: THE MOCHE MOMMY AND MANY MORE MUMMIES

Alva, Walter, and Christopher B. Donnan. "Tales from a Peruvian Crypt," *Natural History* 103(5), 26–35 (May 1994).

*Arriaza, Bernardo. "Chile's Chinchorro Mummies," *National Geographic* 187(3), 68–89 (March 1995).

Dillehay, Tom D. "Selective complexity and adaptive mortuary behavior." Proceedings of the National Academy of Sciences, pnas.org/content/109/37/14722.full.pdf.

*Donnan, Christopher B. "Plain and Fancy: Moche Burials," *Face* 10(1), 30 (Sept. 1993).

*"The El Brujo Archaeological Complex." The English-version website is an excellent resource for learning about the Lady of Cao. www.elbrujo.pe/en.

Maugh II, Thomas H. "1,500-Year-Old Mummy Found in Peru Pyramid," *Los Angeles Times*, May 17, 2006, articles.latimes.com/2006/may/17/science/sci-mummy17.

Norris, Scott. "Mummy of Tattooed Woman Discovered in Peru Pyramid," *National Geographic News.* May 16, 2006, news.nationalgeographic.com/news/2006/05/mummy-peru_2.htm.

*"Why the South American Chinchorro People Made the First Mummies," *PRI's The World,* August 13, 2012, pri.org/stories/2012-08-13/why-south-american-chinchorro-people-made-first-mummies.

CHAPTER THREE: ÖTZI THE ITALIAN ICEMAN

*Brennan, Bonnie, and David Murdock. "Iceman Reborn," PBS's *NOVA*/B Squared Media, aired September 28, 2016, pbs.org/wgbh/nova/ancient/iceman-reborn.html.

*Deem, James M. *Bodies from the Ice: Melting Glaciers and the Recovery of the Past*. Boston: HMH Books for Young Readers, 2008.

Fowler, Brenda. *Iceman: Uncovering the Life and Times of a Prehistoric Man Found in an Alpine Glacier*. New York: Random House, 2000.

———. "Scientists Enthralled by Bronze Age Body," *New York Times*, October 1, 1991, C1.

———. "Should Just Anybody Be Allowed to Stare?" *New York Times*, June 16, 1996, E6.

Haller, Vera. "Modern Marketing Embraces Iceman; Bronze Age Mummy Found on Glacier Moved to Italian Museum Amid Hoopla," *Washington Post*, April 12, 1998, A19.

Klaubert, David. "Wir dachten, das sei ein toter Bergsteiger," *Frankfurter Allgemeine*. September 19, 2011, faz.net/aktuell/gesellschaft /umwelt/oetzi-finderin-erika-simon-wir-dachten-das-sei-ein-toter -bergsteiger-11290181.html.

*"The Making of Ötzi the Iceman." DNA Learning Center, dnalc.org /programs/otzi.html.

*Murdock, David, prod., and Brando Quilici, dir. "Iceman Murder Mystery," PBS's *NOVA*/National Geographic Television, aired October 26, 2011, pbs.org/wgbh/nova/ancient/iceman-murder-mystery.html.

*"Ötzi the Iceman." South Tyrol Museum of Archaeology, iceman.it/en.

Pernter, Patrizia, Paul Gostner, Eduard Egarter Vigl, and Frank Jakobus Rühli. "Radiologic proof for the Iceman's cause of death (ca. 5'300 BP)," *Journal of Archaeological Science* 34(11), 1784–1786 (November 2007).

Spindler, Konrad. *The Man in the Ice: The Discovery of a 5,000-Year-Old Body Reveals the Secrets of the Stone Age*. Translated by Ewald Osers. New York: Harmony Books, 1995.

Wei-Haas, Maya. "An Artist Creates a Detailed Replica of Ötzi, the 5,300-Year-Old 'Iceman,'" Smithsonian.com (February 17, 2016), smithsonianmag.com/science-nature/artist-creates-detailed-replica-otzi -5300-year-old-iceman-180958151.

Wilford, John Noble. "Lessons in Iceman's Prehistoric Medicine Kit," *New York Times*, December 8, 1998, nytimes.com/1998/12/08/science/lessons -in-iceman-s-prehistoric-medicine-kit.html.

CHAPTER FOUR: BOGGY BODIES IN TANNING BEDS

"2,000-year-old bog butter unearthed in Co Meath." *Irish Times,* June 9, 2016, irishtimes.com/culture/heritage/2-000-year-old-bog-butter -unearthed-in-co-meath-1.2678854.

Aldhouse-Green, Miranda. *Bog Bodies Uncovered: Solving Europe's Ancient Mystery*. New York: Thames & Hudson, 2015.

"Bog bodies are kings sacrificed by Celts, says expert," irishcentral. com/news/bog-bodies-are-kings-sacrificed-by-celts-says- expert-129289548-237410131.

*Deem, James M. *Bodies from the Bog*. New York: Houghton Mifflin, 1998.

Dicks, Lynn. "Mystery in the Mire," *New Scientist* 117(2382), 38–41 (February 15, 2003).

Glob, P. V. *The Bog People: Iron-Age Man Preserved*. Translated by Rupert Bruce-Mitford. Ithaca: Cornell University Press, 1969.

*Hart, Edward, prod. and dir. "Ghosts of Murdered Kings," 360 Production for PBS's *NOVA*/WGBH-TV, July 2, 2014, pbs.org/wgbh/nova/ancient /ghosts-murdered-kings.html.

Lobell, Jarrett A. and Samir S. Patel. "Bog Bodies Rediscovered," *Archaeology* 63(3), (May–June 2010).

*Long, Chris. "Lindow Man: Gruesome discovery who became 'international celebrity,'" *BBC News*, August 3, 2014, bbc.com/news/uk -england-28589151.

McGrath, Matt. "World's oldest bog body hints at violent past," *BBC News*, aired September 24, 2013, bbc.com/news/science-environment-24053119.

Ross, Anne, and Don Robins. "Face to Face with a Druid." *New Scientist* 116(1591), 19 (December 17, 1987).

CHAPTER FIVE: ARM TATTOO IN INKY BLUE: THE ALTAI PRINCESS

*Aronson, Marc, and Adrienne Mayor. *The Griffin and the Dinosaur: How Adrienne Mayor Discovered a Fascinating Link Between Myth and Science*. Washington, DC: National Geographic Children's Books, 2014.

Han, Junhi. *Preservation of the Frozen Tombs of the Altai Mountains*. Translated by Lise Sellem and David Tresilian. Flemish/UNESCO Cultural Trust Fund, 69, (March 2008).

*Polosmak, Natalia. "A Mummy Unearthed from the Pastures of Heaven." *National Geographic* 186(4), 84–103 (1994).

*———. Various articles, Science First Hand, scfh.ru/en/all-authors /polosmak-natalia-v.

*"Siberian Princess reveals her 2,500-year-old tattoos." *Siberian Times*, August 14, 2012, siberiantimes.com/culture/others/features/siberian -princess-reveals-her-2500-year-old-tattoos.

CHAPTER SIX: SICK: MUMMY MEDICAL MYSTERIES

Bartholomew, Dana. "'Mummies of the World' exhibit at California Science Center." *Daily News*, June 25, 2010, A3.

Dhody, Anna N. "The Curious Case of Mrs. Ellenbogen." *Expedition* 58(2), 47 (2016).

Habuda, Janice. "'Mummies of the World' Puts Human Face to Exhibit at Buffalo Museum of Science." *Buffalo News*, April 13, 2014.

*"The Lady Who Turned to Soap." Stuff You Missed in History Class, April 13, 2015, missedinhistory.com/podcasts/the-lady-who-turned-to-soap.htm.

Murphy, Jim and Alison Blank. *Invincible Microbe: Tuberculosis and the Never-Ending Search for a Cure*. New York: Clarion Books, 2012.

CHAPTER SEVEN: MATERIAL GIRL IN THE AFTERLIFE: CHINA'S LADY DAI

*Bonn-Muller, Eti. "Entombed in Style." *Archaeology* 62(3), 40–43 (2009).

Chunhong, Yu. "Chinese Lady Dai leaves Egyptian Mummies for Dead." *China Daily*, August 25, 2004, chinadaily.com.cn/english/doc/2004-08/25/content_368631.htm.

Dongxia, Zhang, and Xu Lei. *The Legend of Mawangdui*. Beijing: China Intercontinental Press, 2007.

*Liu-Perkins, Christine. *At Home in Her Tomb: Lady Dai and the Ancient Chinese Treasures of Mawangdui*. Illustrated by Sarah S. Brannen. Watertown: Charlesbridge, 2014.

"T-shaped painting on silk from Xin Zhui's tomb." Hunan Provincial Museum, hnmuseum.com/en/content/t-shaped-painting-silk-xin-zhui's-tomb.

CHAPTER EIGHT: HIGH AND DRY: THE INCA CHILDREN

Brumble, Melody. "Researcher helps unwrap mystery of 3 Incan children." *Shreveport Times*, August 15, 2013, usatoday.com/story/tech/2013/08/15/volcan-llullaillaco-mummies/2660113.

*Clark, Liesl. "Ice Mummies of the Inca," PBS's *NOVA*, originally broadcast November 1998. pbs.org/wgbh/nova/ancient/ice-mummies-inca.html.

Cobo, Father Bernabé. *Inca Religion and Customs*. Translated and edited by Roland Hamilton. Austin: University of Texas Press, 1990.

*Puffer, Brad. "Preserving a Mummy," *NOVA* Online, pbs.org/wgbh/nova/peru/mummies/preservehome.html.

*Reinhard, Johan. *Discovering the Inca Ice Maiden*. Washington, DC: National Geographic Children's Books, 1998.

————. *The Ice Maiden: Inca Mummies, Mountain Gods, and Sacred Sites in the Andes.* Washington, DC: National Geographic Society, 2005.

Wells, Pamela Caragol. *Child Mummy Sacrifice.* (Washington, DC: National Geographic Video, 2010), DVD.

Woodruff, Bob. "Life on Ice: The World of Crazy Cryogenics." abcnews .go.com/Health/life-ice-world-crazy-cryogenics/story?id=14167348.

CHAPTER NINE: THE MEDITATING MONKS: HIDING IN PLAIN SIGHT

Newman, Cathy. "Pick Your Poison—12 Toxic Tales." *National Geographic,* May 2005.

*Squires, Nick. "Mummified Monk Revealed Inside 1,000-Year-Old Buddha Statue." *Telegraph,* February 24, 2015, telegraph.co.uk/news/worldnews /europe/germany/11432544/Mummified-monk-revealed-inside-1000 -year-old-Buddha-statue.html.

CHAPTER TEN: WRAP-UP: THE GOOD, THE NOT AS GOOD, AND THE INFAMOUS

Fraser, Nicholas, and Marysa Navarro. *Evita: The Real Life of Eva Perón.* New York: W. W. Norton, 1980.

*Krull, Kathleen. "Eva Perón," in *Lives of Extraordinary Women: Rulers, Rebels (and What the Neighbors Thought).* Illustrated by Kathryn Hewitt. New York: Harcourt, 2000.

*McCann, Michelle Roehm, and Amelie Welden. "Eva 'Evita' Perón—Actress and Politician," in *Girls Who Rocked the World: Heroines from Joan of Arc to Mother Teresa.* New York/Hillsboro, Or.: Aladdin/Beyond Words, 2012.

*Schmermund, Elizabeth, and Judith Edwards. *Vladimir Lenin and the Russian Revolution.* People and Events That Changed the World, vol. 7. New York: Enslow, 2006.

AFTERWORD

Gill-Robinson, Heather. "Bog Bodies on Display." *Journal of Wetland Archaeology* 4(1), 111–116 (2004).

"Indo-European mummy in the Altai—Part 5." BBC Learning, youtube .com/watch?v=df7ZGHMFtNY.

Lewis, Susan K. "Ice Mummies: Siberian Ice Maiden." *NOVA* Transcripts. PBS airdate: November 24, 1998, pbs.org/wgbh/nova/transcripts /2517siberian.html.

ACKNOWLEDGMENTS

I'M GRATEFUL FOR THE INTEREST AND TIME OF THOSE who helped me flesh out the facts on mummies and provide both solid information and color commentary. To everyone, a heartfelt thank you, beginning with my editor Howard Reeves, who guided me from first draft through final wrap-up.

There are my friends Gloria Lane, M.Ed., and Lisa Lewis, MD, who helped me explain big ideas about biology and medicine to my readers, as did Jolene Pappas, M.Ed. Wallace "Sam" Sergent, PharmD, PhD, assisted with Chinese phrasing. And sincere appreciation to my writing clan: Brandon Marie Miller, Andrea Pelleschi, and Diana R. Jenkins.

To the scientists in my family, from Aunt Kerrie to Christopher German, PhD, of the University of Utah and Mary E. Pendergast, PhD, ecologist with the Wild Utah Project, I say thanks.

Many experts in their fields—sometimes literally—reviewed chunks of my manuscript. Archaeologist Patrick Hunt, PhD, Stanford University, offered valuable insight into Ötzi, the Iceman. Victor Mair, PhD, professor of Chinese language and literature at the University of Pennsylvania, reviewed my chapter on the Tarim mummies.

Anthropologist John Verano, PhD, Tulane University, guided me through the finer points of Moche culture and other burials. Anthropologist Johan Reinhard, PhD, past explorer-in-residence at the National Geographic Society and now an NGS Explorer, offered a wealth of information about the Llullaillaco children.

Julia Farley, PhD, and Daniel Antoine, PhD, of the British Museum offered careful observations about Lindow Man. Ole Nielsen, director of the Museum Silkeborg, shared his knowledge of bogs and the bog body Tollund Man. Vincent Van Vilsteren, curator of archaeology at the Drents Museum, brought me up to date on Yde Girl. Emily Snedden Yates, MFA, museum special projects manager of the College of Physicians of Philadelphia, and forensic archaeologist Kimberlee Moran, M.Sc., RPA, at Rutgers University clarified details about the Soap Lady.

I'm very grateful to archaeologist Jane Hickman, PhD, of the University of Pennsylvania Museum of Archaeology and Anthropology and editor of its fine *Expedition* magazine.

My thanks to anthropologist Margaret Bruchac, PhD, of the University of Pennsylvania, who addressed my concerns about the continuing questions of culture and context in studying indigenous peoples.

Finally, to my agent Jeff Ourvan, my thanks for leading me to this project and also serving as my go-to resource on Buddhism.

PICTURE CREDITS

INDEX

Note: Page numbers in *italics* refer to illustrations.